52 Weeks of Passion and Pain

52 Weeks of Passion and Pain

Journey of a Wounded Soul

By

Anita Lorraine

Copyright© 2017-Anita Lorraine

All rights reserved. This book is protected by the copyright laws of the United States of America. This book may not be copied in whole or in part, nor may it be reprinted for commercial gain or profit. The use of short quotations is both permitted and encouraged. Otherwise, any reproduction of this material in whole, or in part is prohibited without expressed permission from the author.

Front cover photo: Lewis Duval Photography, Philadelphia, PA

ISBN 978-0-692-99250-0

DEDICATION

This book is dedicated to:

<u>My children</u>, Aaron and Adonijah. You are the reasons I live. You are my pride and joy. You love me unconditionally and inspire me to be more and do better. You give me purpose. I see the good parts of me in you and I am persuaded to believe you can accomplish anything. Since I see it in you, I must see and believe the same for myself. I'm not the best mother. I may not even be a good one, but I hope one day I make you both proud to call me your mother. I love you endlessly.

<u>My mother,</u> Mary. You are my rock, my number one intercessor and my biggest fan… Without you there would be no me. You demonstrate strength and courage daily with a faith in God I have never seen waiver. You epitomize godly character and when it comes to mothers, God gave me the best. You always have my back. To be half the woman you are will be an awesome accomplishment for me. I love and appreciate you more than I will ever be able to express.

<u>The memory</u> of my grandmother, my cherished cousin, my goddaughter and my little sister; Elizabeth, Roberta, Nayyira and Olivia. Never did I think a day would come when I wouldn't be able to share such a monumental occasion with you. Because of who you all were, I AM. The wisdom in your words, I still hear. The love you had for me, I still feel. I can only hope you felt that same love from me before closing your eyes. My love for you remains. You are irreplaceable in my heart. I hope you dance.

<u>Every person</u> who has experienced rejection and sexual abuse: every child who's been molested, everyone who was raped, every man, woman, boy and girl who was ever inappropriately touched or mishandled, those who had the courage, strength and support to make it known and

especially those who did not, for every encounter exposed and hidden, every tear shed in secret or openly acknowledged, this is for you.

<u>Anyone</u> who knows or has known the pain of not loving yourself. May you find the courage, grace, wisdom, strength and peace to completely love who you are. I hope you are one day able to see yourself as God sees you and embrace all that is you. Even if you don't feel it, I love you.

<u>You</u>, who thought it not robbery to pick up and read the pages of this book. May you find some piece of encouragement, strength and, or wisdom that will inspire you along your own journey.

"Death and life are in the power of the tongue: and they that love it shall eat the fruit thereof". Proverbs 18:21 (KJV)

"Words have both creative and destructive power. I choose to create."

-Anita Lorraine

CONTENTS

Foreword..13

Disclaimer...15

Introduction..17

PHASE 1

A Stroll Down Memory Lane.................................27

Ode to Mufasa..34

Tweener..36

Runaway...38

Dear Tooty..40

EAGLE...42

Mirror, Mirror..43

Her..45

Underland...48

And Then..49

PHASE 2

Growing Up in His Shadow....................................51

FAITH..54

Sin…………………………………………………………………..55

Pond Water…………………………………………………………..56

Seed………………………………………………………………...57

Dear Nita……………………………………………………………59

Dry Place…………………………………………………………...63

Into Me See…………………………………………………………66

Green Eyed Monster…………………………………………………69

Alphabet Soup………………………………………………………70

<u>PHASE 3</u>

Her Death Gave Me Life……………………………………………73

Freedom song………………………………………………………75

A Mother's Heart……………………………………………………77

Grief…………………………………………………………………79

It Wasn't a Dream……………………………………………………80

FOCUS………………………………………………………………84

My Sweet Anita Lorraine……………………………………………85

Unknowing…………………………………………………………88

Revoked Innocence…………………………………………………90

PHASE 4

Punishment..91

Civil War..98

Reflection...101

Lies..104

Misery Loves Company...105

Honesty...106

Letters to Love...107

My Secret..110

The Ugly Duckling...112

Christ Must...113

PHASE 5

Hospital Horror..121

GREATER..129

Falling High...130

Once Upon a Time...132

Liar, Liar..133

Philly..134

Into Light Before Death...136

Phantom...139

PHASE 6

The Demon Who Started It……………………………………..141

A Packaged Deal……………………………………………..146

Self-Destruction……………………………………………..148

Stilettos……………………………………………………..149

Passion and Pain……………………………………………..152

Afterword……………………………………………………...157

FOREWORD

In a day when many get their inspiration from superficial statuses, filtered pictures and unrealistic expectations; Anita Lorraine dares to share the true sentiments of her heart. Her raw transparency is sure to touch the core of your soul and bear witness to the fact that the beautiful tapestry of life consists of the good, the bad and the ugly. It is my prayer that you are encouraged and motivated to soar as you journey through these beautiful writings that have been delicately woven together to tell her "beautifully messy story".

Apostle Kim A. Davis

Senior Pastor

Ebenezer Full Gospel Baptist Church

River of Life Church

Founder/CEO

KAD Ministries

DISCLAIMER

*The stories within these pages are true to the best of my knowledge. Some names have been changed to protect the identities of the innocent.

**Some of the contents of this book are considered extremely graphic and may not be suitable for children under 17.

INTRODUCTION

You may be thinking, "why should I read this book?" "What makes her story so special?" Why should you be interested in reading pages from the story of my life? The answer is simple. It's inspirational and empowering. It's interesting. It's honest. It's real. Although it's tragically poetic, I cannot say that my story is unique. Unfortunately, it is a story that is far too familiar to far too many. You may find yourself amidst some of these writings. I cannot tell you that you will find the answer to overcoming pain. You will not find a magic solution to heartache. You will not find an equation to solve life's dilemmas. What you will read are the sentiments of my heart. You will read of my failures. You will read of insecurities and lack of confidence. You will experience my passions. You will feel my pain. You will journey to the highs of my victories and sink to the depths of my defeat. You will read about how I experienced both the best and worst times of my life congruently. You will learn of the power that lies within YOU to be more and better than you may think you are capable of being in this moment.

This book began as something I just wanted to accomplish. I hadn't thought about publishing. So I certainly had not thought about sharing with the world. I just wanted to finish the dang blasted thing. I looked at my life and concluded that my greatest achievements are my children. While they will remain forever at number one, I didn't -in my own twisted opinion- have anything else that was good to show for my life. A severed marriage. Failed attempts at business endeavors. No money. No house. No car. Increasing debt. Bad credit.

Materialistically I had nothing to show for my life. While I wanted to put the blame on others, and could justly do so in some cases, the fact of the matter is that at the end of each day, I was the only one who kept me from doing the things I desired to do. So it was important to me to finish something. I needed to.

I used to be intimidated by people who have the same gifts as I do. The way I used to view myself kept me from launching out to turn my potential into promise. I would look at others living out the things I desired to do and I would shrink. I shrank because I never felt like I was good enough. I never felt smart enough. I never felt pretty enough. I never felt popular enough or supported enough. I never felt like I was enough, period. In recent days a fierce jealousy arose in me. It wasn't because I was "hating". I was quite proud to see so many people from my community doing such great things. I was jealous because I saw other people doing what I KNEW I could do, and in some cases, better. So I decided to join the ranks of achievers.

I was raised in church. So I have it perfected. I know how to move a congregation – I'm gifted in exhortation. I know the Bible. I know what to quote to get a specific response from the crowd. I know when it's a good time to "cut a step". I know how to "hype" a preacher. I have spent all of my life in church. That means I have also done all my dirt, IN CHURCH. I would sit in service after service getting so much word. I was spiritually fat. I received and received and received. I poured into people I was comfortable with. I only shared with people who thought like I did. I shared with people I knew would receive me. I was terrified of rejection. I became a people pleaser, in a sense. With all the practical steps I had been taught on how to be and do and live better, I didn't because I was fearful of so many things.

Whenever I write, I can be or do or say whatever I choose. I have no limits. Just my thoughts and a blank canvas. It's the one place I'm never judged. I'm never scolded on right versus wrong. I'm never laughed at for messing up. I'm never condemned for falling short. I'm never looked at funny for expressing the true sentiments of my heart. I'm never challenged for speaking my mind. I'm fearless when I write.

I discovered something I know I am good at. It's something no one can take credit for teaching me. It's something I enjoy as much as breathing. It's a gift, given to me by the Creator, Elohim. I just want to share it.

I remember my first time at the Writer's Forum at "The Spot". I was invited by my cousin, "Bert". I had written a poem just for the occasion, but I couldn't find it when it was time to go. It was a Wednesday evening. I was 13. I walked to "The Spot", now known as the Coatesville Cultural Society and wrote another poem, just like that. It didn't have a title, but that day, I remember feeling like, "I'm pretty good at this poetry stuff".

"When the weight of the world is upon my shoulders

And my heart is heavy like stone

When I've done everything in my power

Working my fingers to the bone

What do I do where do I turn

Peace of mind is what I yearn

But when will it come

Must I continue living in fear

In times like this I need a friend

One who will stay near

God promised he'd never leave me

That he'd always be there

Sometimes I have to wonder

Does he even care

His gentle response was enough to help me face the day

His blessed assurance was strength enough to carry me all the way

So here I stand as a soldier

In the army of the lord

I'll fight the enemy until he gives in

Or dies by my shield and sword"

When I found that poem years later and read it as an adult, it made me think of all the things that made me feel like I was carrying the weight of the world. You would think a 13 year old doesn't have a care in the world. Some may not. I had many. I recall one commentator asking what I knew about being in an army and carrying a shield and sword. All I knew was what I had learned about the Holy Bible being a sword and my faith being a shield. There was song often sang in church about being a soldier in the Lord's army. Somehow I felt that I was supposed to fight this "enemy" who weighed me down. I remember the precise issue I was facing at that age. To me, it was the end of the world. My mom was about to get married and I would no longer have her to myself. I was going to inherit another dad and more siblings. At the time, I didn't want that.

I listened carefully to what each individual had to say about the piece I had written. I received a few critiques, but I did not feel criticized. Overall, it was enjoyed. I liked the thought of my words having the power to make people feel good. I enjoy knowing my words make people feel anything at all.

While I can say that I have been inspired by a few well known greats such as, Dr. Maya Angelou, Edgar Allen Poe and Langston Hughes, my greatest inspiration comes from people I know personally; my family and friends. Women and men I have the liberty and pleasure of speaking with and interacting with on a regular, if not daily basis. Reading their words, drinking in their wisdom and watching their lives unfold before my eyes has fed and inspired me more than the pages of any book I've read, written by the hands of those I don't know.

Several years ago, I began an autobiography. For weeks upon weeks, I wrote. It flowed out of me like water and I was very excited and full of hope. Then, devastation hit my marriage. My life began unraveling at the seams. It contradicted everything I was putting on paper. All of the beautiful things I had said about being married and pursuing my dreams were becoming more foreign as the days passed. Although the words I wrote were at one time very true, I didn't know how to turn the corner from that place in my writing. I had a block and I couldn't write anymore. I tried to force something, but nothing would come to me. I didn't know which direction to go. I didn't know how to get my flow back. I didn't know how to tell the story anymore. So I quit. Much like everything else in my life, I got mad and frustrated and just gave up. For several years after, I didn't write. I had so much to say about so many things, but I could never bring myself to express them. Oddly, not being able to write affected my ability to verbally communicate. My thoughts I could hear clearly, but I was unable to transport them from my mind to my mouth. I didn't lose my ability to speak, but I lost my voice.

One day, I was reflecting on my experience with a past lover and my heart was overwhelmed - so much so, that I began to cry. When the tears wouldn't flow any longer, I began to write. Just like that, it was back. As I read the words on the paper, I could hardly believe I had written them. I knew then, that I would write poetry. I couldn't finish the autobiography because I wasn't supposed to write it. I have always known I was supposed to share my story with others, but I limited my audience to people I knew and was comfortable with. It didn't become clear to me that poetry would be my vehicle to a more broad audience, until the moment I absorbed that piece.

I didn't know where to begin really, except to just write what I felt. So that's where I began. As I continued to complete piece after piece, it dawned on me that I didn't have a title for my project. I pondered how many writings would be suitable. There were two things that were very evident in my work. I had experienced a fair amount of passion and I had experienced a fair amount of pain. The passion I speak of in these writings are not directly related to the things I am passionate about. It is more about what I experienced emotionally and physically. So, "Passion and Pain" was originally what I came up with. There still lingered the question of how many poems I needed. What would make it complete? My partner and I bounced a few ideas around. There are 365 days in a year. That was far too much. There are 12 months in a year. That was far too few. There is an average of 30 days in a month, but that didn't feel right either. We looked at one another and at the same time said, "52". There are 52 weeks in a year. It was perfect.

The idea then, was to write one piece per week. So, I decided to call it "52 Weeks of Passion and Pain". In theory, my idea was flawless. In reality, it was much more challenging than I had anticipated. Thinking I could just spit out 52 personal, detailed and intimate writings like it was nothing was a delightful ambition I fell terribly short of. It has taken me longer than 52 weeks to finish this book. Initially, the number 52 was supposed to just be a reasonable number of poems and stories to complete my project. I only wanted to share it with a select few. I wasn't ready to expose myself. I didn't think I could handle putting my life on the chopping block and allowing anyone who wanted to, take a stab.

It turned into more than a year of internal reflection. I took a journey into myself to unveil all the things I had bottled inside. I sat with myself and thought about who I was and what I wanted. I thought about what I used to have. I thought about what I gave up. I cried over some of the things I walked away from. I pondered all the ways I've experienced passion. I smiled at the thought of being able to do the things I enjoy. The things I'm most passionate about are writing, doing hair and baking. They have at times kept my sanity. I also smiled at the thought of having experienced such pleasure my body could hardly contain it.

The bible says, "Death and life are in the power of the tongue: and they that love it shall eat the fruit thereof". (Proverbs 18:21) I have been fortunate enough to taste the fruit of life. I endeavor to share that with others.

I thought about all the things that have brought me pain and those to whom I have caused it. Being able to admit that I have caused others pain hurts my heart. I have only ever desired to please. My pride and ego would have kept me blind had I allowed them to. They would not allow me to admit, let alone express my faults. I wanted to see the truth. I needed to. The only way I knew to achieve that was to look in the mirror and be brutally honest with myself. It has been a painfully difficult, yet very rewarding journey. There were truths about myself I was unable to face prior to this journey. Some of them are very ugly. Since I have taken such a long look in the mirror, it has been so much easier to accept myself. I don't feel burdened to change based on the belief systems of others - only my own. It also doesn't hurt when other people point things out that they see, because I already know it's there.

    I noticed as months passed, that my work had become more intimate than I intended. They weren't things I thought off the top of my head, though I am well capable of producing such. They weren't surface readings. They have depth and substance. They aren't all rhythmic. They don't all rhyme. They aren't all pretty. They are emotional. They are gut wrenching. They are pleasant. They are graphic. They are painful. They are tear-jerking. They are real. They are thought provoking. They are spiritual. They are inspirational. My life has been a combination of all those things. If you know me, you may even catch the humor sprinkled throughout. They tell a beautifully, messy story - MY story. So, come. Let's journey through 52 weeks and see what we find.

"Untamed. Freedom is your mantra. You are music. Life is your song."

-Anita Lorraine

A STROLL DOWN MEMORY LANE

"Nita, you can be the cat." Or, "Nita, you be the baby." Those were my answers to the question, "Can I play?" I knew neither of these characters had speaking parts. Yet, I consented to the role. As a little girl, I liked to watch my older cousins play. More than I liked to watch, I enjoyed the rare moments they let me participate. I remember one game in particular. Before "Barbie", there was "Barrettes". I didn't quite know how they remembered which barrette was who or which color did what. They made it look like the most fun game in the entire world. I wanted to play.

I loved my cousins. They were more like the sisters I never had - Kalia and Bert. I always wanted to be like them, follow them around, and do what they did. They were so animated and creative. They had a way of turning what seemed to be nothing, into something so spectacular. I wanted nothing more, than to be a part of it. I didn't care if I was the cat, or the baby. I didn't get to talk and interact much. I can't say that I was totally okay with that. I just wanted to be included. So, for the sake of *being* a part, I *played* the part.

Then, there was a force called, "Falert". If you knew Falaq and Bert, you know exactly why I said, "force". Being with those two together was a guaranteed adventure.

Let me just say that although I know my cousins loved me, I don't know why I liked them so much. Sometimes they were SO mean. One time, they took possession of MY doll and I had to get permission from THEM to play with it. How twisted is that?

Back to "Falert"... We used to play "house". Not the inappropriate kind, the innocent kind. Bert was always my mom. She named me "Tammy". Every time we played, that's how I wanted it. We played "dress up". They made up all kinds of fun games. They were smart-mouthed and very sarcastic, but so much fun to be with. Sometimes I couldn't tell if they were being funny, rude or just making fun of me. I loved them though. I thought they were "cool as jaxx". I always wanted to be included in what they were doing. My older cousins were a major influence in my life.

Bert is the reason I enjoyed "Tuesday Nights" and I will not drink milk if it hasn't been shaken. Falaq is the reason I made dresses out of my Auntie's sheets and wore colored yarn in my hair. Kalia is the reason I like "poor man's chicken" and always wanted to "wrap" my head and wear "racy" clothing. Mary Alice was NOT having it. To this very day, they all still influence me and impact my life in a positive manner. They have challenged my thinking and inspired me to be more open.

I believe at some point in life, everyone has experienced a desire to "belong". It stems from the basic need for human interaction. We all want to be a part of something. Desperation and insecurity have at times, gone hand in hand in my attempts to fit in. I used to agree to anything if it meant being a part of SOME thing. It wasn't until my early 30s where I didn't desire the pursuit anymore. I have completely given up on the pursuit of acceptance. Instead, I accept that I will never belong. No matter how hard I try, my square just will not fit into anyone's circle. I don't blend. I was born to stand out. I'm perfectly okay with that.

I am not fortunate enough to recall the first few years of my life. I know some people who are. I can only trust what I've been told by my mother and family. One of my earliest memories though, is one of rejection. I was about four years old. I remember my mom telling me that my dad was coming to see me.

I don't know how many times he had been there before. I had seen a few photos of him and me when I was little. My favorite picture was of him holding me atop his shoulders. We were standing in the middle of my grandmother's living room. My dad and I were both showing our pearly whites. It made me feel that whatever was happening in that moment, we both enjoyed it. We looked happy.

All I knew is that he was coming to visit. I was so excited. The day seemed to drag on. My dad couldn't get there fast enough. I didn't know anything about time. I didn't know if there was a certain time he was supposed to show up. I didn't know if the arrangement was for him to come in the morning, noon or evening. Whenever it was, he didn't show up. That began a search within me for something "wrong".

My mother and grandmother, affectionately called "Grandmom" raised me. All the love and care they displayed, all the time they spent with me, all the walks they took me on, all the stories they read, all the times they tucked me in, all the lessons they taught, all the meals they prepared, all the shopping trips, all the vacations, all the toys, all the clothes and shoes... None of that seemed to matter when I felt let down by my dad. Even the times he did come through were insignificant in comparison to when he didn't.

Why is it that bad seems to outweigh good? Think about it. It's like, no matter how much good a person does for you, that one bad thing, that one hurt, that one disappointment, that one rejection does far more damage than can be repaired by a few good deeds. Right? That couldn't be further from the truth beloved. Those negative things have only the power yielded them by you. You can choose to forgive. You can choose to release. It's not always easy and there may be some cases in which you are justified not to. However, the reward of freedom is so much better than the weight of a grudge.

I took a faith based course called Elijah House in 2008, via New Community Christian Church. In that course I learned that the men and women we grow to be are a result of who and what we are taught we are during the first 6 years of our lives. Our basic trust is founded during these years as well. God designed the system of (immediate) family to consist of father, mother and children. Not all families are built that way. Our instruction and guidance as children should have come by way of God's original design. We all did not have the luxury of mother and father. Some have only mother, or father. Others have grandparents or aunts and uncles. There are some who have two mothers or two fathers. I didn't know the joys of having both a father and mother in the home until I was thirteen, when my mother married my step-father, Daryl Washing Sr. Nonetheless, however we were taught in our early years, by whoever taught us, we learned. Those lessons came from the things we saw, the things we heard, and largely, the things we felt. All the elements of our environment and instruments of our earliest education combined to create a belief system.

Due to my early and continued experience of what I interpreted as rejection, I believed that something in me was not good enough. My belief system was that I had to earn my way into love and acceptance. I had to do something in order to be accepted and included in the lives of the ones I loved. Every form of rejection from the first moment I felt it, further fed that belief. Each time I wasn't included or accepted strengthened the hold that false belief had in me. In addition, my basic trust was damaged.

I didn't trust people in general. I didn't trust them to accept me for me. I didn't trust that they wouldn't let me down. I didn't trust that they wouldn't hurt me. I figured all this out as a child. Of course in my early youth, I was unable articulate such feelings and beliefs. Yet, somehow, I was able to express them. I didn't trust that my cousins would let me play if I wasn't the cat or dog or baby. Instead of telling them I didn't like those roles, or simply asking for another role, I shrank. In exchange for inclusion and the feeling of being accepted, I played a part I didn't really want. I felt it was my only way "in". I was not always allowed to play with my cousins, though. There were times when they told me no.

My eldest cousin on my mother's side, Kalia, affectionately known as "Pooda", to this day, still tells me about how I would stomp my foot and cry in an effort to make them let me play. She said I sounded like the siren of a fire truck when I cried. I do remember doing that. It makes me laugh because I remember the sound of my own voice back then. I did indeed sound just like a fire truck. To this day, sometimes when I hear the blaring sirens of a fire engine, I reflect on my childhood and smile. Pooda is an awesome story teller.

While my little tantrum didn't always get me in their games, I did get my mom's attention. I learned that having somewhat of a fit may not have gotten me what I wanted at that moment, it always got me attention. I remember my mom wrapping her arms around me in an effort to sooth my mood. She had a way of making me feel like I was the only person in her world though I shared her with so many. She was always there for me – my mommy. I am her only living (birth) child. I believe she felt that she had to make up for all that my dad didn't do - whatever "it" was. I don't know if it was because he didn't want to or wasn't able to or just forgot to. From where I sat, he mostly didn't. I and my mom both paid for it.

When I was around three or four my dad got married. I don't remember the wedding but I do recall the reception. I remember the look on my dad's face that day. I had never seen him with such a big smile. I danced with my cousins. I had 3 cousins who were all the same age as me. They were boys. We played well together. I liked wrestling them because I usually won. That day, there was no wrestling. We ate cake and ran around the reception hall, taking turns chasing one another. I liked the woman my dad married. She was nice. I don't, however, have any memories of her prior to her union with my dad. We'll call her Lucy, but I called her "Me-Me" for a very long time. When I grew to appreciate the role she played in my life, I started calling her mom. That's what she was to me, a mom. About two years after they got married, I had a baby brother. I used to watch Me-Me nurse him. I kept wondering why she had him under the blanket. I asked one day what she was doing and she said, "Feeding him". I didn't know the proper term back then. I liked my brother. I used hold him with my step-mother's help. He was cute and had big ears. I enjoyed being around this little person.

    I wonder how you'd look at me if I told you that I spent time locked in a basement or got beat with a broom when my dad wasn't around. You'd probably cringe if I told you she used to throw shoes at me or burn me with cigarette butts. You would probably feel moved to feed me if I told you she used to send me to bed hungry or didn't bathe me. You could experience some nausea if I told you she made me sleep with the dog and eat out of his dish. You might wanna fight her if I told you she talked reckless about my mother.

    Although tales of a wicked step-mother would make for a more interesting read, that isn't my story. I love Lucy. She has never laid a hand on me except to love on me. I know there were times she wanted to though. My mouth? My sarcasm? My attitude at times? I'm almost embarrassed to admit how "bad" I was. "Mom" never made me feel unimportant or nonexistent. She always included me. People who didn't know her personally, she would tell, "I have 3 children". She never said that I wasn't her child. I remember a few times she would say, "this is Carl's oldest". She NEVER disowned me though. She never treated me badly.

    It seemed though, that I spent less time with my dad and more time with Me-Me and my baby brother. I didn't mind. I remember lots of cook outs and barbecues in the big yard. (I still haven't figured out what the difference is between the two.) There were frequent visits from various friends and relatives. She was ALWAYS taking pictures. Sometimes we took trips to visit other people. My dad was not always there. He was either working or sleeping. I always felt like a part of his world when I was there, even if he wasn't.

A few years after my brother, another baby came. I had a little sister. Pretty much the same thing that I went through with my brother, occurred when my sister arrived too. I was older by then and could help a bit more. I didn't have any negative feelings towards my sister and father until she got a little older. I noticed that my dad called her "Badness". It was a name he only called her. I wanted one though. I was always just "Nita". On occasion he called me, "Lorraine". Both were my birth names that my mother gave me. They didn't seem very special to me at that time. Now, I wouldn't trade them for the world. I rather enjoyed being a part of two different families. I loved my family. I still wanted nickname though.

I asked my dad one day why he didn't have a special name for me. We were standing outside by the back door of the house. He told me, "L. Boogie" is my pride. He is my first son. "Badness" is my joy. She is my BABY girl. ...but you, Nita, are my pride AND joy. You are my first born. No one can take that from you." Now, I don't know if he was blowing smoke because he hadn't given me a nickname, but every fiber of my being totally believed him. Not long after that, he started calling me "Little Rain". I liked it. No matter what my siblings were called, they were my world. I was their big sister. I loved it. I lived for the weekends at my dad's.

ODE TO MUFASA

You are the image of a perfect medley

Your Majesty

You command respect of your audience

In just the way you move

Your mane

Full luscious and thick

A crown fit for a king

Your eyes are the lyrics

They speak when there are no words

With sight beyond the natural realm

The way you walk

Composed of strength and grace

The melody is in your every stride

Your voice pierces the silence

Wisdom

Floods out as a song

Your sound is flawless harmony

Sweet

To the ear

Your hunt is a measure

Calculated

Timed

Though quiet and still for a moment

Rhythm without error is

Your pounce and capture

Untamed

Freedom is your mantra

Swiftly you defend your pride

Your harem

Your den

One fierce roar is like a thousand trumpets

A strong blow

The veil between life and death

Torn

There is a hush

Rest

You are music

Life is your song

TWEENER

My nose was big and my lips were small
I wasn't really short and I wasn't really tall
I never hung out or sat with the popular crew
I wasn't liked by everybody only by a few
My clothes were thrift shop brand and I didn't mind
Mommy always got the best she could find
The boys called me names some of the girls were mean
I ditched school sometimes just so I wouldn't be seen
I used to lick my lips and had a scar around my mouth
I used to wish I never had to leave the house
Don't even get me started on the stories of my hair
I used to like it until the kids would talk point and stare
I had bad skin that I used to try to scrape away
I hated looking at my reflection every day
Mommy said I was beautiful because she was supposed to
Believing it was an occasion that I eventually arose to
Not fully being one thing, but not really being another
On one hand I'm an only child on the other sisters and brothers

I'm a square peg in a world that is round

Most times by myself is where I can be found

I had to learn to appreciate how God created me

Self-discovery has been a rewarding journey

I didn't have a hard life but it was still hard

Now I'm aware of just how to play my cards

RUNAWAY

I see the tears in silence you cry
I know the pain you try so hard to hide
I see your wounded and tattered heart
If feels like your world is falling apart
I know deep down why you are sad
What you did you wish you never had
I know what it is to feel completely alone
Thinking everything you do is absolutely wrong
I feel the fear you don't acknowledge that you feel
Please take my hand and let me help you heal
I have dealt with the raging storm you feel inside
Please give me your bag and let me help you fight
I've many times said all the things you now frequently say
You don't really want to leave, you just want the pain to go away
I see your bag and I know you're ready to make the run
Leaving the situation doesn't mean that you've won
Surrounded by people but you feel like you're lost inside yourself
You're smiling outside while internally screaming out for help
Open your door and let me in if only for a day

I promise you'll no longer feel the need to run away

The place you are now you feel forever stuck in

Every place you've visited I have already been

No one should do life alone angry rejected bitter and hurt

I will help you find your way out I'll help you do the work

Dear Tooty,

    I am you, a little more than 30 years from now. I want to talk to you for just a few moments. You will be going to school soon. You will not make many friends. You will be loved by your teachers though. You are such a sweet girl. You want everyone to like you. The sad truth is, they won't. A few will, but the ones you want to like you most will be the ones who do the most damage to you. Don't let them.

    Your mother worked very hard to make sure you know how loved you are and how special you are. She will always tell you that you are different. Don't view that as a bad thing. People don't always understand different and sometimes they even fear it. You will never get everyone to like you. Don't try to be a people pleaser. You will fail miserably. Be confident in the words that your mother affirms you with. Walk with your head high. You only need to respond to people who echo your mom's message to you. Whatever you do, please don't pick up other people's habits to make yourself fit in. You may at times be WITH the crowd, but you will never be IN the crowd.

    You just don't belong, baby girl. Don't be afraid to be the one to stand out in the crowd. Don't let what other people think of you change the way you go through life. I remember one particular incident where you were in school. Grandmom had pressed your hair and gave you tight curls. You wanted a style like your older cousins', but yours was different. You liked it a lot. You spent so much time in the mirror looking at each curl. You were amazed by Grandmom's ability to take your curly hair, make it straight, and then style it with those small curlers.

    You bounced down the hallway on your way to your classroom with such joy and pride in your new do. Until one child said you look like a grandma with all those tight curls. As other children laughed along with her, you shrank a bit. You still liked it though. At recess, it happened again. Your smile turned into a frown and the hairdo that you loved so much became the bane of your existence.

You tried to laugh along with them. You didn't want them to know they were hurting your feelings. Inside you didn't understand why they were being mean. You would never say the things they said to you. That was the beginning of your ability to wear what I call "the game face". Instead of telling the other kids that you liked your hair, you minimized yourself and Grandmom's hard work.

Please, my little one, be brave. Be strong. Be courageous. Speak up for yourself. Don't let anyone steal your voice and don't let them make you wear a game face. Instead, change the game. You are different and different is good.

I love you Tooty.

Your older, wiser self.

EAGLE

Effortlessly rising above storms we
Avail ourselves to the sweet currents of the wind
Gleaning strength and beauty from the Son
Leaning into the grace of each new day
Excelling in the flow of the oil in our wings

MIRROR, MIRROR

Self-transparency.

Being see through with self.

Not just seeing all the aesthetically pleasing

Beauty but acknowledging

All the unpretty

Unflattering

Unattractive

Unspeakable

Things in one's own self

It's uncomfortable

Forced to confront

The choice presented

To evolve

Or remain the same

And risk swiftly becoming irrelevant

Perfected game face beguiles

One into believing they're actually alright

Can't be big

And little at the same time

Stretch

Face the truth

Accept it

Or reject it

It's still there

There it will be

On the wall

Staring at me

HER

This girl right here with the smooth soft mahogany skin
This girl right here with almondy eyes that draw you in
This girl right here with the bright smile and seductive grin
This girl right here is fighting demons within

This girl right here with her body so tight
This girl right here with her make up just right
This girl right here with her stride so light
This girl right here weeps through the night

This girl right here in every way is unique
This girl right here is not known in the streets
This girl right here doesn't fear her own beat
This girl right here doesn't get invited to meets

This girl right here wears her heels to the sky
This girl right here has her own kind of fly
This girl right here struts with her head held high
This girl right here is really very shy

This girl right here is intelligent, bright and witty

This girl right here has a way about her that's nifty

This girl right here is funny and at times downright silly

This girl right here doesn't think she's very pretty

That girl over there looks in the mirror with a new found grace

That girl over there likes the look of her pretty face

That girl over there checks for insecurity but there's not a trace

That girl over there is winning her race

That girl over there is living life like she has it together

That girl over there smiles through all kinds of weather

That girl over there is free now that those soul ties are severed

That girl over there thinks her life has never been better

That girl over there appreciates the sway of her hips

That girl over there likes the way her back dips

That girl over there kisses deeply with her small lips

That girl over there so full of love it drips from her fingertips

That girl over there cries real tears of joy from her soul

That girl over there breathes life to those who have grown cold

That girl over there has a story that's never been told

That girl over there has no fear of the vast unknown

That girl over there understands what it means to live free

That girl over there has copious roots beneath her tree

That girl over there completely accepts who God created her to be

This girl right here is that girl over there and that girl over there is ME

UNDERLAND

All the pieces of a heart that's been shattered can be totally made whole.

A person can live in the belly of a great fish for 3 days.

A child's lunch can feed over 5,000 people.

Animals can talk.

Fish have money in their mouths.

Washing in dirty water heals diseases.

God is the glue that holds me together.

God will sustain me in my darkest, most lonely hours.

God is the source of my supply He takes my little and makes it much.

God will speak to me any way He sees fit I have to be open to receive the unusual.

God alone will be able to get the glory for my success and prosperity.

God can heal me spiritually, emotionally and physically without use of conventional means.

In Underland, nothing is impossible and with God all things are possible… only to them that believe.

Do you?

AND THEN

She made countless mistakes.

She looked at herself at times, as nothing more than a failure.

She often questioned God. "Why am I here?"

She never settled herself long enough for an answer.

She spent many nights turning and tossing, tossed and turned.

She experienced frustration after frustration.

She endured disappointment after disappointment.

She cried through situation after situation.

She began to enjoy the journey into herself.

She learned how to still herself and commune with her Creator.

She freed everyone of all rights to her joy and success.

She released herself of her own perceived failures.

GROWING UP IN HIS SHADOW

As I got older, I was able to call my dad on my own and schedule visits by myself. I would ask my mom when I could go. Then call my dad to make sure he could come pick me up. He worked at the Veteran's Administration Hospital near our house on Coates Street. I was smart enough to know, only because I memorized how to get to his house in Avondale that he had to pass Coates St. to get there. So, in my tiny mind, I couldn't understand how he could ever forget to pick me up. Was I that unimportant?

The usual summer arrangement was for him to pick me up Friday morning when he got off at 7. My stepmother, Me-Me, would drop me off Monday morning when she went in. During the school year, Me-Me would pick me up on Friday when she got off at 4. Then Sunday night, dad would drop me off when he went in at 11. It was the perfect arrangement.

One memory sticks out in my mind. It was a turning point in my young life. It changed the way I behaved when it came to my dad. I called my dad to arrange a visit. He agreed to pick me up. As usual, I got excited. I packed my weekend bag and was ready to roll. By then, I knew full well how to tell and keep time. I knew my dad got off at 7 and that he would be there no later than 7:30. Friday morning my mom made sure I was up. She had braided my hair and put lots of beads in. I LOVED when mommy put beads in my hair. I was ready to go by 7. I sat my bag by the door. I stood in the window where grandmom had a tree stand that was full with pictures on each shelf. I peered out the window looking for my dad's blue Chevy. Grandmom was sitting in her chair in the living room and mommy was on the couch under the big mirror. I kept looking out the window. My little heart raced every time I heard a car coming up the street. None of them were my dad. I paced from the window to the clock and back to the window. I did so for what seem to be hours. We weren't allowed in that window. Grandmom didn't want her pictures disturbed. Under other circumstances, I would've been told to get away from her tree. Not this time though.

The last time I checked the clock on the wall, the little hand was on the 8 and the big hand was on the 4. I knew that it was 8:20. It was almost an hour past time for my dad to have been there. I called his house. I had memorized the number -268-3433. That was before we had to dial the area code first. He answered the phone much to my dismay. The excitement I had felt earlier seemed to drain all at once from my little body. "Daddy, I thought you were coming to pick me up?" I tried my best not to sound sad or disappointed. I fought off my tears so I wouldn't make him up upset, or disappointed in me for not being a big girl. His reply shook my entire world, "Aww, I'm sorry Nita. Daddy forgot". How can you forget your daughter?! My eyes swelled with tears as he explained that he would pick me up the following weekend.

I had already bragged to my cousins that I was going to visit my dad. I told my best friend Myesha who I played with every day. My bag was packed. I will never forget the feeling of my little heart breaking. I said my goodbyes and ran into my mother's arms. I buried my face in her bosom as the tears streamed down my face. I kept repeating myself, "He forgot me. He forgot me. He forgot me." My mom held me tight as I continued to sob. She spoke softly to me and I felt a little better. I walked over to grandmom, who was crocheting. I knelt down at her feet and put my face in her lap. She rubbed my back and said some encouraging words.

From that day, I made a vow not to ever let my dad forget me again. I would make myself just like him. I would like what he liked and do what he did. I was sure that would solve his memory lapse. I learned that my dad liked ketchup on his scrambled eggs. I started eating my eggs with ketchup. My dad loved horror movies. I would watch them with him and not let him see how afraid I truly was. I grew to like them. My dad liked roller coasters. So, as soon as I was big enough, I would ride with him. I felt good about that because my sister and brother were still too little. It was something only me and dad could do. Dad liked sports, so I played basketball when I really wanted to be a cheerleader. I wasn't even that good a ball player, but the first time was the last time he ever saw me on the court. To me, it was worth the sacrifice. For a few years, my plan seemed to work. Eventually, I did grow into my new practices and they became my own likes and desires.

FAITH

Flee disbelief

Act as if you have it already

Inoculate doubt

Trust in the Lord who

Hastens to perform his word

SIN

It is universal...from the white house to the crack house...from your house to my house...from the wolves on Wall street to the fiends in the darkest alley...everyone is guilty...because the first man fell, we all felt it...thanks to Jesus, it was brutally dealt with...now I have a right to the Tree of Life...I'm making my mark and shining His light...I'm way far from perfect and not afraid to admit it...I'm on the Potter's wheel and He has a whole lot to work with...I gave Him my life under a vicious attack...now I'm doing my best not to take it back...people and things try to move me, BUT I'm not moved by what I see...I fall down occasionally and scrape my knees...then I fall to my face, ashamed at their success in budging me...what got me down may not be your snare...your life to mine, I'm not trying to compare...just want to help you see...sin is universal...be careful how you judge me.

POND WATER

I wasn't dying but I wasn't living

I wasn't coming but I wasn't going

I wasn't blind but I couldn't see

I wasn't deaf but I couldn't hear

I wasn't numb but I couldn't feel

I wasn't dumb but I couldn't speak

I wasn't lost but I couldn't be found

I wasn't anything but I was something

What frightening place to be

Just there

No one to throw pebbles into the center

Making ripples

Just stagnant

Stinking

Taking up space

SEED

If you only had a dollar, would you give me fifty cents
Holding on to your last, like that's as good as it gets
Afraid to let it go, because your thoughts are so corrupt
I'll let you in on a little secret; it'll help you get your game up
The Creator gave us gifts, based on the body's needs
He tells us to be fruitful, and multiply our seeds
All of us don't listen. We're ashamed of our talent size
So instead of experiencing increase, we permit our seeds to die
Spying on our neighbors who appear to have more than we
Our hands go up in despair, and agony of defeat
If we would take some time to sweep our own front door
We'd have no to time for obsessions of who has more
These very precious gifts, entrusted to our hands
Are meant to bring healing, deliverance and prosperity to the lands
Our focus, far too frequently is zoned in on another
That usually causes tensions and discord amongst each other
Look into your hand and cherish what the Master bestowed
Don't put that seed in the ground for there it will surely not grow
Saturate it with the Father's love and faith

Bury it in His spirit, and it will germinate

The talent that's been given, should be appreciated by you

For what you have is a mission only you can do

Weather you have five talents two or even one

Take your gifts and double them for you've been empowered by the Son

Dear Nita,

    There are so many things I would like to say to you. I can't though. You seem to know everything already. You hear a lot, but you don't listen. I'm too old to waste my breath. I'm not old at all, actually. Life has taught me a lot and wisdom has grown me. So, I feel a bit older than I really am.

    At this age, you are going to go through more than is absolutely necessary for you. Your parents love you. They are doing the best they can with what God has given them and you should be helping them. You are making it difficult. You are not the only one your decisions affect. You have younger siblings who look up to you and memorize everything you do and say. I want so much to tell you not to leave. I want to tell about how hurt your brothers will be. I want to tell you about the conversations your mom will never have with your dad because she misses you so much and wants to rescue you. She won't, because she knows there are lessons you have to learn that she cannot teach you.

    You are beginning to "smell" yourself. Guess what? You stink! I know you don't think so now, but you will know one day, just how badly you do. You aren't a bad girl. You aren't disrespectful. Which is why I'm having a difficult time totally understanding why you aren't receptive to what your parents are trying to tell you. I get it. You have been with your mom without interference for 13 years. It has been just the two of you. I understand, believe me, I do. Didn't you pray for a dad though? Didn't you tell God you wanted a father? I know you meant your biological father. I think all kids want both of their parents to be together. That's honorable. When you were old enough to understand why that wouldn't happen, you changed the way you prayed. God honored your prayer the same year you prayed it. How awesome is that? God heard you and He responded. You are pissing on His gift with your disrespect.

    Want to know something else? I know you really don't, but I'm going to share anyway. You feel like you are betraying your "real" dad somehow. You love Daryl and you are afraid he will actually be the dad you want and need and that scares you. You think you're going to forget about Carl and he will somehow feel abandoned. I want so much for you to let that go and embrace the gift God has given you. I also know that you struggle internally with your respect because of the things you have seen Daryl do and heard him say. Unfortunately, you don't get to choose whether or not you honor your parents. You are blessed to have FOUR of them. You are obligated to honor them all. You can't pick and choose. Especially since you asked for it.

      You're going to go live with your dad and your step-mom for one school year. You will learn that the grass is not greener on the other side. There are rules everywhere you go. Your stepmother's rules are much stricter than your mom's. You can't even go to the park without your brother and sister down there. *sigh* Nita, I urge you to think before you act. Sure, you'll meet new people. You'll make new friends. You will take on this "bad girl" persona and get into a bit of trouble. The crowd you choose will lead you down a path that will cause you more pain than is necessary. You have only yourself to blame for that. You'll get it together by the end of the school year though. In the summer, you'll go back home to Coatesville. Then, two years later, you'll do it all over again. Only, the next time... Please, Nita, I'm begging you to reconsider. I see down the road. I see where you are headed. You are going to be heartbroken. The real world is nothing like the world you see in your head. Unless you choose to be led by the wisdom of God, you will learn that the hard way.

Sneaking out of the house late at night?? Yeah. You'll do that at the suggestion of one of your associates. Going to go see some grown man who needs to have his ass beat for letting you come over there. He doesn't "like" you. In his eyes, there is only one thing you can do for him. It's only God's grace, your mother's prayers and your guardian angels that he kept his hands to himself for as long as he did. When you gave him the "okay"? SMH. I wish you hadn't. He'll be a bit of a problem for you later on in life.

Not only will you be sneaking out of the house, but you'll steal your mom's car to impress a bunch of people who really don't give a damn about you. You'll change the way you dress. You think sexy is in your attire and you couldn't be more wrong. When I think about all the things in your life that COULD have gone terribly different with all the stupid things you'll do and irresponsible choices you'll make? I can't help but thank God for his unmerited favor. The part that really makes me sad is that none of this is YOU baby girl. All this just to fit in and sadly you never will. The sooner you learn to love yourself the way God made you, the better off you'll be. You're hard headed. So you'll do things your way and learn the hard way.

  I will tell you though, that the horrible things you will encounter are going to keep you from taking an even more dangerous path than the one you are choosing now. They will draw you closer to the father you asked for. You will have a bond with him that is impenetrable until the day he closes his eyes. You will make him and your mother proud. Yes, I said you will encounter some horrid things. It isn't necessary for you to go through what you will soon face. It will however, make you better. Stronger. Wiser. More respectful. It will humble you. It will do for you, all the things your parents were trying to do before you started "smelling" yourself.

  Aaahhhhhh.... I have your attention now. You'd like to know what will happen, huh? I'm not at liberty to say. It will change your life though.

  You are fortunate to have such a loving supportive family. Not everyone can sing that song, my dear. Cherish your family, from the very least in age, to the greatest. They will not all be with you for all your days. Don't give them your ass to kiss. They don't deserve it. You owe it to yourself not to be "that girl".

  I love you. I can surely say that you will be okay. You'll be better than okay. I just wish you didn't have to take the road you are taking. You only HAVE to take it because it's the path you are choosing. Only you have the power to change your course. You will not though. You're stubborn and like to learn things on your own terms. I respect that.

Peace be your journey my love.

Love always, yourself

DRY PLACE

Across the land I
Walk and feel the scorching heat
I'm in the desert

I need refreshing
Allow me drink from your well
I will never thirst

This is my journey
I did not choose this dry place
Still it is my lot

The sun burns my skin
No trees to give me relief
The wind blows hot sand

If fire had smell
I am the definition
But don't smell like smoke

Precipitation

Held hostage by the heavens

I need refreshing

Uncomfortable

I live this environment

Daily hot and dry

My feet are burning

If I had wings I would fly

But I must march on

Endure this hardness

The season will change again

I need refreshing

The sun disappears

Clothed with strength in the dark hours

Rest for a moment

I'm in the desert

I will not die in this place

I'm fit to finish

INTO ME SEE

What do you see when you look at me?
I don't think you truly see me when you look at me.
So I'd really like to know what you see.
You said you're spiritual, but how can that be?

How can you look in my eyes and not see clearly?
Why can't you tell I'm not free?
I'm a spirit. I have a soul and live in a body.
Why does your spirit not connect with me?

Is it because you don't really want to see?
All I really need is a little intimacy.
I suppose you just don't have the time to be with me.
You don't have space in your life for all my negativity.

Maybe you aren't equipped to handle the ruined places in me.
I'm really not asking selfishly.
I'm asking you because there truly is a need.
What do you see when you look at me?

I don't want to hear that I'm shapely and pretty.
I've perfected the appearance of the outward me.
Something inside longs to be set free.
All I really need is a little intimacy.

How come when I'm falling no one hears me scream?
Behind my flawless smile and perfect stride I'm really weak.
My skin is raw from wiping tears but my Maybelline is all you see.
I'm all beat up and I wanna fight but I'm afraid to get on my knees.

You only look at the outward me.
I need help with what's happening inwardly.
You don't have time to deal with me.
Well will you talk to God about me?

Will you at least pray with me?
All I really need is a little intimacy.
I'm not talking about, "oh Father we thank thee".
I mean the kind where you push until you feel something happening.

I need that place where chains are broken and demons flee.

I know I'm a huge responsibility.

You won't be sorry if you invest your time in me.

It's silly of me to even think you have the energy.

Someone told me I'm worth it and I want to believe.

If you could just look past the outward me.

Please?

All I need is a little intimacy.

GREEN EYED MONSTER

There used to be something inside of me. It was an awful monster. There were so many things I wanted to do and be. So many places I wanted to go and stuff I wanted to see. I kept listing all these hindrances making excuses for things I should have could have and would have done. At the end of the day looking in the mirror I found only one.

ALPHABET SOUP

I'm

Astronomically above average,

Bred for blessings,

Cancelling out carnality,

Detrimental to demons,

Equipped with excellence,

Focused and flossin' without fear,

Giving God glory,

Heavily hammering haters,

Ignoring ignorance

Flowing colder than February with extraordinary grace.

I'm so peculiar.

I'm

Joyful over the love of Jesus,

Kingdom minded and conquering with kindness,

Living life out loud and loving it,

Motivated to move in ministry,

Nocturnally knocking out evil on my knees,

Opposing the norm operating in love and wisdom,

Prayerfully and peacefully parting ways with my past,

Quietly praying for my enemies,

Rejoicing over restoration

And walking in purpose with passion daily!

I'm such a royal priesthood.

I'm

Strategically living,

Totally transforming into greatness

Understanding first before seeking to be understood,

Victoriously vacating unhealthy vices,

Washing and wallowing in wisdom

Xeroxing myself to reproduce greatness

Yearning for all God has for me,

Zealously zeroing in on His will

And maximizing every moment life has to offer!

I'm so chosen

HER DEATH GAVE ME LIFE

There she is, lying on a cold table. She lived so many years of her life in fear. Intimidated by false evidence appearing real, she forgot everything and ran. She feared what people thought about her. She was afraid of what they might say. She was intimidated by the possibility of her success. She feared failure. So, she lived a mediocre life. She wanted to blend. She desired to belong. She just wanted acceptance. She didn't pursue her dreams. She shunned the thought of the responsibility that came with being great. Being the woman she had seen in her dreams seemed unattainable. Now, she is dead.

She was a people pleaser. At any moment she would drop anything of her own concern to make others happy. She lived to see the smiles she was able to bring to others. She was always willing to support and push others into destiny, all while hers gradually slipped away. Without two of her own nickels to rub together, she found ways to be a blessing to others. Sadly, it never truly satisfied her.

She died a slow and very painful death. She was not surrounded by loved ones. No one was present to see or catch her tears. There was no comfort from the arms of a lover. No sweet, whispered prayers of her mother. She was alone. She didn't want to be. She didn't want to go out that way. It had to be. She screamed at times until her throat was sore. Other times her eyes would swell shut from tears cried in silence.

She was a great pretender. Her bright smile masked years of pain and agony. Her laugh offered an impression of sheer joy. She had a way about her that made people feel at ease. While inside of her was turmoil, raging. A storm of emotions churned within. Clashing seas of bitterness, anger, jealousy, hurt, envy, pride, insecurity, fear and inadequacy fought with who she truly desired to be. She was a liar. She was a master of deception. Until one day, she grew weary of the struggle and killed herself.

She was a sweet girl, truly.

She is survived by one brave, courageous, fearless woman. That woman walks in freedom in honor of the life of bondage that was laid to rest. That woman is, me. She killed herself and now I live in a confidence I have never known. She laid herself on God's altar of sacrifice and I got up as the new creature. I allowed God to fill the cracks of my soul and mend all the broken pieces of my heart. I called back all the scattered pieces of myself and He has made me whole.

I live in the joy of the Lord, knowing full well that He perfects the things that concern me. He has revived the ruined places in me. He caused the heart of my dreams to beat again. He has breathed life into my visions of success given by Him. My passion for God has been reignited and the flame burns fiercely. I am in hot pursuit of my destiny. I made a choice to face everything and recover. I am finally free.

FREEDOM SONG

My heartbreak broke me

But it woke me to an incomparable possibility

The possibility for me to be completely free

To release every inhibition that bound me

I fell hard

I was in the dark

And when I hit the bottom I was exposed

Every part of me

Was open

The light poured in

Everyone could see my sins

I thought I was for sure damaged goods

But it was for my good

Being abused mistreated and misunderstood

If there was no fall I couldn't have risen

My eyes would never have opened

And wouldn't have otherwise seen that I needed to be forgiven

Easy it was to forgive everyone else

The true test came in forgiving myself

I was open

And broken

I was openly broken

But the light came in

I could finally see

It poured in

It shined out

It was all in me and through me

It surrounded me and guided me

My heartbreak didn't damage me

It ironically made me free

I'm open

I was never broken

I can't express

The joy I feel in this new liberty

What used to be a mere possibility

Is now my reality

I'm open

Not broken

That means I'm free

A MOTHER'S HEART

I did what I thought best for them and it turned out to be the wrong choice for me. I wanted so much for them to be with both of their parents. That just wasn't going to be.

Only a child can break a mother's heart. Ask me how I know. My children broke mine.It wasn't intentional, I'm sure. In fact, they don't even know, but was only a matter of time.

I have often been torn in processing the hardest thing I have ever had to do in my life. Between facing my dad in court and letting go of my babies? Neither one of them was right.

On one end of the spectrum is the one who took part in creating the mess that is me. On the other side are the masterpieces I co-created. Two perfect, innocent little beings.

I'm in the middle. Caught in a storm. All the pain I carry myself. The tears I cry unseen. This is my punishment. I'm being reprimanded for decisions I made when I was just a teen.

Only a child can break a mother's heart. Ask me how I know. My children broke mine. It wasn't intentional, I'm sure. In fact they don't even know, but it was only a matter of time.

If I could turn back time to the day I told their father, "Yes, they can go with you". They wouldn't be calling someone else mom. Or face days where they feel they have to choose.

They broke my heart. I know they didn't mean it. They were so little, innocent and cute. I never wanted them to know what it is to struggle. I didn't want them to be broken and confused.

Only a child can break a mother's heart. Ask me how I know. My children broke mine. It wasn't intentional, I'm sure. In fact they don't even know, but it was only a matter of time.

I chose to let them go away from me. I chose to leave them in their father's care. Never wanted to be one to separate a good man from his children. I knew they'd be safest there.

I wasn't mentally, spiritually or emotionally fit to give my babies what they needed and deserved. The choice I made didn't even become real until divorce papers were served.

Actually, my children did not break my heart. The situation they have been forced into has been no easy feat. They are my every heartbeat. It's just... their absence makes me feel incomplete.

GRIEF

There is silence in the walls of my city

No warmth is left in my sun

No chirping in my birds

No song in my breeze

My streets no longer are filled with laughter

The children are gone from me

Quiet and still are the once rushing waters within my gates

Sleep toys with me

I seek

And it hides

Their sweet whispers haunt me

The glory of their smiles is ever before me

My moon is pale

I taste the sting of frozen air

Bitterly greeted with the cold of winter's chill

Come to me Spring I beg of you

IT WASN'T A DREAM

Yup

He came knocking

So I let him in with his tall

Fine

Smooth self

And his handsome

Crooked grin

He took me in his arms

He held me close and tight

The whisperings

In my ear

I melted right into him

I didn't put up a fight

He wined me

And dined me

He played with me

He sang to me

Promised that wherever I went

He would find me

His words dripped

Into my ears

Like honey

I was falling

Fast

I wanted someone else to catch me

Anyone

But him

I couldn't get away

From

That moment

Felt so good

I was slipping from myself

Wrapped up

In his embrace

Why did I want to escape

He was well dressed

All in black

I was consumed by his presence

I danced with him that night

Feeling weightless

As we moved

He closed my eyes

Gently

I felt his breath on my neck

I knew this

Was taboo

Somewhere

In me

Had to be

Courage

To say no

As I felt him reeling

Me closer

I pulled his hands away

He pulled me back in

I can't do this

I know it's a sin

It was my place

I had to put him all the way out

He smelled so good

He said everything

Right

He was strong but gentle

I wanted to go

All the way

I could no longer

Resist the fight

I was mad

Why did I let him in

With his tall

Smooth

Fine self

And that handsome

Crooked grin

Almost went

For that long

Hard ride

But I kicked him out

Last night

I almost committed suicide

FOCUS

Freedom from things that otherwise

Occupy the mind of Christ in us, we are liberated from

Cumbersome burdens and delivered of

Unproductive thoughts and behaviors

Solely fixing our sights on the prize

My sweet Anita Lorraine,

I'm probably the last person on earth who should tend a garden or take care of any type of plant life. To leave greenery with me is a sure fire death sentence. I have a black thumb. I have some knowledge, but am far from gifted in the application thereof concerning plants. I do know however, that if one does not prune a plant, it will surely die. The pruning process involves a cutting away of the dead parts of the plant, or the parts that are not growing with the rest of the plant. It is an absolutely necessary process. A plant that is not properly pruned is destined to die.

I'm not much older than you are now. I have been exactly where you are. Pruning is paramount for you. It will hurt, but you will be so much better. Just go through the process.

Can you imagine if we had to physically endure a pruning process? Suppose you'd have to lose your left index finger in order for your legs to gain strength needed for walking. Or what if you had to have your right arm amputated because it was keeping you from being able to speak? What would life be like if you had to choose between having your sight or your hearing? What if you had to lose your tongue for your fingers to grow and function? I'm sure we would meet a lot more physically challenged people than we already do. We would have to choose which parts we were willing to function without, in order to operate at maximum capacity. Take a moment and think about what YOU would look like.

Consider how disfigured you may look mentally and emotionally. Have you ever just looked at a person and said to yourself, "they have some serious issues."? It is quite obvious the way some people move through life, that they have some serious things going on. If you can tell that just by looking at some people, what types of opinions are they formulating based on the way you move through life? Do you move as if you are holding on to dead weight? Do you speak as if you have venom flowing through your veins?

I was forced to take a look at myself. In a dream, I saw an image of myself. It was sickening and disheartening. I looked a mess. I was missing fingers and toes. There was a hole where my heart should have been. My eyes were completely black. I had chunks of meat missing from my body. I looked like I had been attacked by a wild animal. My left foot was depicted as an anvil. Just horrific. It was graphic and looked like something that was taken from a horror film. I had to ask God what each thing meant and how I was supposed to go about changing it. Most of it was corrected by the pruning process. Some people and things just had to go. Did it hurt? Absolutely. It didn't happen overnight. I had grown accustomed to going through life being so severely disfigured. Those people places and things that were represented in that image of myself had become my crutches. They were my friends. I confided in them. They bore my secrets. They held my faults, failures and insecurities. Surely I couldn't let them go. I'm here to let you know that if I had not pruned them, I would have surely died.

    The pruning process for me was one that I didn't want to make. Not because I didn't want to be or do better. I didn't want to inflict pain on myself. I didn't want to be accountable. I just wanted God to take it all away. That way, I'd have someone to blame later down the line when I felt I needed something that had been removed. That is how so many people are, and why so many have not experienced freedom or healing. We want someone else to do the work. I had to make the choice myself, FOR myself. When I finally began the gruesome process of cutting away, I felt an assurance that I would never again return. No matter how appetizing those things may appear to be - and at times they are quite attractive - I will NOT go back. I am able to call to my mind what I endured to experience freedom and I refuse to repeat the process.

    There is something about an appreciation for doing something yourself. If someone just gives you a car, you are a lot less likely to take the same care and concern for it than if it were a vehicle you had to work and save for. When I think about the times I asked God to take something away from me, and He did, more often than not, I returned to that thing. However, the things that I had fight through, the things I cried through, the things I prayed through, the things I wrote through, the things I had to sever MYSELF, were more appreciated. Don't get me wrong. I absolutely am grateful for the things God took away from me when He took them away. The fight and determination I produced during my battles though; left an indelible impression in my heart and mind. Some things I just REFUSE to rewind, repeat or replay.

By the way, I am you. Happy. Healed. Whole. Prune what you know you can. Allow God to do the rest. You will only achieve victory when you fight for it. It will not be gift wrapped and handed to you on a silver platter. You shall not die, but live!

I love you more now than I ever have.

Signed,

A wiser, braver, better, stronger, YOU.

UNKNOWING

I'll take off all my clothes

Let you watch me delicately remove each article

Turning every motion into a dance

Every dance gracefully tells a story

Your heartbeat quickens

Your breathing intensifies

Piece by piece my clothing falls to the floor

It gently lands at my bare feet

Your wide eyes take in my ample breasts

Strong shoulders and firm arms

My flat stomach and narrow waist

Child-bearing hips

Perfectly rounded behind

My thick thighs and toned legs

Down to my perfectly polished toes

Your eyes tell me I'm beautiful

They say you thirst for me

You are hungry for this experience

I come to you from across the way

Sauntering

So as to momentarily draw out your longing

Your fingers gently dance across my mahogany skin

Your lips sing to mine

A familiar taste

A familiar song

A familiar embrace

You pull my hair with excitement

My response raises your intensity

We have perfected our routine

You're no stranger to this nude work of art

You are the only one in my gallery

And when you leave

I cry because you've never seen me naked

REVOKED INNOCENSE

I was robbed. He came for my stuff. I knew who he was. He didn't ask for it. He gave no notice of his arrival. He was not invited. He just showed up. He took my stuff. It was all I had. He stole it from me. I was powerless to defend it. My stuff. He got it and I can't get it back.

PUNISHED

October 15, 1995 was a day I shall not soon forget. There I sat at the desk of the Officer Chesco. I had been asked the question all night, but hadn't offered an answer. Now, it was presented again - "What happened?" I was only 15 but I had been undesirably thrust into a very grown up situation. I had to talk like an adult- use "adult" words. It was time out for baby stuff. Mom and daddy weren't there to coddle me. Only the hand of a red headed stranger held mine as I looked into the kind eyes of the police officer. Marleen Miller was her name –the lady who sat beside me. I had only known her for several hours. At that moment, she was my best friend. I really wanted my mom. I wanted her gentle voice to reassure me. I needed to feel her loving arms wrapped around me. I was scared. I didn't know what to expect.

Couldn't he just get the story from Auntie or Evelyn? I couldn't say it. It didn't feel right crossing my lips. I didn't want it to be true. If I said it, it would be just that. Nonetheless, I swallowed hard and began that horrid journey.

It was dark. It was hot. I slept on a mattress supported only by the floor in the master bedroom of the house. I shared a room with my baby cousin. Her playpen was on the opposite side of the room. I had a little white alarm clock on the floor. It was under the window next to where I lay my head. I kept it there so I could hear it and get ready for school in the mornings. I was a hard sleeper like my dad, and I snored… like my dad. I would sit the clock in the window facing the light for a while. I'd turn it toward the street lights so it could charge. The numbers and hands on it glowed in the dark. The light was faint, but the clock read 2:40. It was the wee hours of the morning. I wore blue pajamas that night. I was missing my mommy. Blue was her favorite color. Somehow, they made me feel connected to her. I was lying on my stomach. My face was turned toward the clock. I had my left leg clocked and my right leg extended. My arms were supporting my head. I didn't have a pillow. It was hot up there.

  I hadn't been living there long. I had been sent to the office for cursing out a teacher earlier that day. My parents did not tolerate disrespect. That day, three of my parents had been called into the principal's office. Mary, Daryl, and Carl had been alerted of my actions and were summoned to decide my fate. It wasn't' the first time I had gotten in trouble in school, but it wasn't a regular or normal thing for me to disrespect those in authority. My issues were usually with my peers. My mommy and daddy looked very hurt and disappointed. My dad just looked. I couldn't determine what his eyes said. I listened as each of my parents offered their opinions as to what should be done regarding my punishment. When it was all over, I had to leave school. I had been suspended for a day. The following day I would return to Coatesville Area Senior High School. I was expected to offer an apology to the faculty member I had so brutally disrespected in front of everyone. Before we all left the office with that understanding, mommy and daddy verbally expressed their disappointment in me. I fought back the tears. I couldn't let them see me cry. I hated hurting them. I had to prove a point though. To this day, I still don't know what that point was. My dad, Carl, had very few words for me. He simply said, "I'll deal with you later." I chuckled to myself thinking I'd get off scott free. None of my parents had ever successfully punished me. Well, except maybe my mom, and that was before she married daddy. My biological father, Carl, had only ever put his hands on me one time. A few licks to me and my cousin Vinny with a belt, and we were back outside in no time. My feelings were more hurt than my butt.

  I was sleeping lightly when I heard him give his goodnights before coming up the stairs. He went in the bathroom. I could see the light go on when he went in. I heard the toilet flush, the door opened, then off went the light. I heard him go in his room. It was right next to mine. I closed my eyes and drifted back off to sleep. My slumber was disrupted by his cough. I had heard it a million times. The smoker's cough. It sounded painful. Moments later, I had an eerie feeling- like someone was watching me. I heard the floor creek a bit. He stood there for a few minutes. I closed my eyes and pretended to be sleep. I even threw in a light snore for plausibility. As I lay there, I wondered if he had a beating brewing for me. I suddenly remembered his words to me before we left the principal's office earlier that day. Surely he wouldn't wake me from sleep to make good on that promise at such and odd hour. I squeezed my eyes tight as I listened to him walk into my room. My heartbeat quickened. Perhaps he was just checking on the baby. I thought I was done for. I was in for the beating of my life. I felt him on my mattress leaning over me. My heart raced and pounded hard. It felt like it would beat clear out of my chest. He reeked of beer and cigarettes. I continued playing possum. I tried to control my breathing. I didn't want him to know that I was really awake. I could feel heat radiating from his hands. He slowly and carefully slid his fingers under the elastic bands of my underwear and pajama bottoms. A sudden heaviness came over me. It was as if an elephant had just sat on my back. He began to gently tug at my bottoms. Unable to get them totally down the first time, he smoothly guided my left leg to a fully extended position. With my legs now parallel to one another, his job was downhill. He removed the lower portion of my clothing.

    The sound of my own heartbeat was deafening. It was all I could hear. My thoughts collided and clashed in a frenzy of my trying to fathom what was taking place. I kept thinking I should be doing something. This was that moment in the movie when I'd remark about what I would do if I were her. I'd yell at the TV screen urging her to do something. "Run girl!" "Girl you better get up!" "This girl is dumb." Now that I was that girl, I didn't know what to do. I couldn't move. I was paralyzed with fear. How was I supposed to keep this from happening? I didn't know exactly what was happening, but I didn't like how it felt. It made me feel alone. It made me feel afraid. It made me feel weak. I don't recall hearing him undo his pants. I don't recall any sounds he made prior to touching me. All I could hear was my own heartbeat and my thoughts that seemed to be screaming at me. Whether or not he had pants on when he walked in, I may never know. I just know when he climbed on top of me, they weren't there. The left side of the mattress shifted downward. He was positioning himself over me without putting his weight on me. I was terrified. My heart pounded fiercely. So much so, that I thought for sure he could hear it. As I felt his body get closer to mine my eyes swelled with tears. Then it happened. The minutes that passed thereafter seemed to linger indefinitely. It was as if time forgot to do the one thing it was ordained to do, move. All at once everything slowed down. Each second procrastinated before passing to the next. He took his fingers and played with my vagina. At first it was just one finger, then two. He whirled them around inside of me. On the inside it felt like a dance. My body liked it. I remember feeling my clitoris swell. Then it throbbed. It seemed to beat in time with my heart.

  I couldn't make my body understand that this was an improper response to such a devious act. It was the same feeling I got the first time I had ever laid eyes on pornography. I was 12, but had a friend who was older than me. Her mom had movies. After school, while our moms were both at work, I'd go to her house and we would watch them. She had a big screen, floor model TV with a VCR on top. She would pop in the VHS tape. I'd sit on the edge of the bed eagerly consuming what my eyes beheld. Those scenes were filled with things I never imagined I'd ever do. I enjoyed watching nonetheless. When I looked at them, I recall a feeling between my legs that made me want to do what the people on the screen were doing. When I got older, I understood that I had been sexually aroused. I never told anyone.

He pressed the head of his penis against my outer labia. He rubbed it up and down. I felt his hand around his penis between my legs. His hands felt rough and hairy. He managed to slip his head in the small slit that lead to my vagina. My lips were open and I wished hard for them not to be. My thoughts were yelling at me. Kick him! Move your legs! Get up! Run! Hit him! Holler! Roll over! Bite his arm! Scream fire! Say something! Do something! People will always run to watch a fire burn. My body failed to respond to any of these commands. He pushed slow and hard. I tensed the muscles in my thighs. I thought perhaps he would be alerted to me being awake and jump up. Much to my dismay, he proceeded. He wiggled his dirty dick left to right and pushed some more. He pulled back a bit and made small circles across my inner labia. He pushed again. And again. And again. And again. His first few attempts were extremely uncomfortable, but I felt no pain. The little resistance I was offering had begun to work against me in the form of a terrible cramp. The little fight I put up was totally ineffective. With one final, hard push he broke through my defense. Immediately I felt pain. One forceful thrust had won him the prize. I opened my mouth to scream but I heard nothing. My voice had somehow escaped me. I cried out for help. Still, no sound was heard. It was as if someone snatched my voice from my throat. By now, the tears were running from my ducts like a steady faucet stream. From my left eye, across the bridge of my nose, in and out my right eye, down the side of my face and dripping down my arm, they pooled on the sheet beneath me. I think the pain I felt was a piercing of my soul, not the penetration of my young vagina. I tried to kick but my legs felt like lead. My arms felt glued to the mattress and my head was glued to them.

    In my mind I was fighting. In reality, I was doing nothing. I couldn't move. I was letting it happen. Why should he have stopped? Why didn't he stop? Couldn't he tell I didn't want this? I felt him remove his hand once he was firmly planted inside. With every onslaught I felt him dig deeper inside me. I wanted this assault to end quickly. I stared into the clock. Then, through it. The minute hand had barely moved any. I thought hours had passed. He groped my breasts underneath my pajama top. He continued his vicious pursuit. The hair on his thighs felt different on my thighs than did the hair on the base of his penis that scratched my tender skin that barely had hair. The scent of smoke and alcohol oozed from his skin and breath. It made me sick to my stomach. I wanted to vomit. I asked God to please help me. I was saying it with my mouth and yet nothing came out. I wanted to be rescued. I wanted someone to come to my aid. I wanted someone bigger and stronger than him to throw him off of me. I wanted God to do that for me. That was the help I was looking for. That was the help I was expecting.

Instead, I had an out of body experience. I had often heard of them when people were close to death. I didn't want to die! Ironically, I felt like God heard my prayer though I uttered no audible words. My grandmom and mom had always said that God was always on time and that He'd be there when I needed Him. Though I strongly perceived He was late, I couldn't think of a better time that I needed him. As I squeezed my eyes tight, praying for rescue, my body went limp. Physically, I no longer felt anything. I didn't feel the weight of him on top of me. I didn't feel his hands roaming my body. I couldn't feel his penis maliciously probing my vagina. I felt like I was floating. Somehow I was looking down on him. He rocked himself back and forth atop my tiny frame. He was a man. I was just a girl. I was his baby girl. I was his first born. Was this real? Was my father really raping me? The same man who had consensual sex with my mother 16 years prior was now on top of me. I was watching a horror film and I was the star. Looking on, I appeared to be dead and he was very much alive.

Immediately, without warning or a notice of some kind, I was forced back into my body as he withdrew his penis from me. I don't remember him getting up. I don't remember hearing him pull up his pants. I don't recall hearing the sound of a zipper. I don't remember too much of anything he did when it was all over. I just lay there. All the thoughts that seemed to be barking commands had come to a screeching halt. I could no longer hear the thud of my heartbeat within the walls of my chest. Total silence. I felt empty. I felt abandoned. I felt abused. I felt betrayed. The punishment didn't fit my crime. His words resonated in my head "I'll deal with you later". He had certainly held up his end of the bargain. The tears continued running. I felt a dull throb between my legs. It was unlike the throb of my clitoris. It was like a pounding headache that somehow made its way to my vagina. My insides hurt. I felt crampy –like I was having a period. My nipples were tender and sore. Strangely, I felt that God had answered my prayer. I asked Him to help me, and he did. He didn't allow me to experience all the physical pain of the ordeal as it happened. What I felt afterwards though, would follow me for the rest of my life

CIVIL WAR

    Blissfully caught up in a whirlwind of deceit, I didn't know what was coming for me. Nothing mattered except what I wanted and thought I needed. There was a gaping void in me and I was obligated to feed it. I wanted to do what looked good felt good tasted good and smelled good. I was big and bad and smelling myself so I did it all. Forsook the call, let pride rule and not long after came my fall. I had ceased getting on my knees and it made me weak. I lost my seek and I couldn't speak. My eyes swelled with tears and all I could do was weep. There was a war within me. I was both winning and losing. I could have ended it simply by choosing who I would serve. I just kept refusing. Accusing and blaming everyone else. All the while I knew who the adversary was really using.

    Trying to serve God and the flesh baby it just doesn't work. You can only love one, the other you'll have to desert or you'll end up hurt. I was a flirt. I flirted with death and I almost died. I danced with manipulation and masqueraded in lies. "When you know better, you do better." That isn't always true. 'Cause I knew, but I didn't do. Instead I offered up every kind of excuse. "It's either me, or you." Hearing those words solidified the fact that I had to choose. I didn't want to do it then. I needed more time. That thing played real heavy on those heart strings of mine. It was titillating and illuminating and somewhat liberating. Yet at the close of each day I found myself frustrated.

    I kept searching inside and all I could see was smoke. I found vows I had made as a child and they made me choke. Swallowing my own words I was disturbed and annoyed and somewhat confused. Everything I felt was clashing with what I knew and every day it grew. I felt terribly misguided, misunderstood and misused. I had become the devil's muse. I had a front row seat to my own demise. My vice was my disguise. I turned into what I had once despised. There was nowhere to run and no where I could hide. I didn't have it in me to fight. I wanted to die but I was afraid to take my own life.

I would hesitate to placate; not ever knowing what I was going to get. Some days I would titivate myself only to find myself by myself to stimulate myself. I'm not just talking sexually. I'm speaking of my esteem. The way I viewed myself? I couldn't really see. I needed much help. I was defining myself by the opinions of everyone else. I knew I couldn't stay, but I didn't want to leave. I tried to cleave but all roads pointed to an inescapable heave. The things that once brought me pleasure felt like chores and I wanted nothing more than to endure this hardness. I felt secure 'cause I knew what every day was hittin for. I guess God felt it was time to end the war.

All the things that were wrong had turned into right. I had no sight, couldn't hear and could muster no might. I was living on the prayers of the righteous and found my way back with their light. I had buried mine deep within. With all my sin I was certain I'd never see it again. God had a plan and I didn't understand why he wanted me. I no longer wanted myself. How could I possibly be wanted by someone else? I looked inside and there was dust all in me. I stilled my thoughts and I could hear a faint, "trust me". A few words, "God, help me". I was rusty and not sure why he still loved me. Prayer was what I knew. So that's where I began. He opened a door and I took his hand.

The devil had me in his clutches and he should have killed me. He's not very skilled. See? He has no new tricks. He gets his kicks on rewinds, replays and repeats. I didn't get it at first, why he wanted to slay me. It was because of my awakening. I started coming into knowing exactly who I am to the King. I'm his child. I have dominion and authority. He gave it to me. Now not only do I see, but I know and believe. I'm a threat to the enemy. I'm a slayer. I see into his lair and go after the kind that go out only by fasting and prayer. He tried to use my heart to destroy me and he almost got his way. God had the final say. Now today I'm awake and ready to make the devil pay.

    I didn't have a handle on my identity. I'm a spirit. I have a soul and I live in a body. My flesh is always fighting against who I truly am. So I have to kill it. Live in the spirit and I won't fulfill my own lusts. Communion with Almighty God is an absolute must. I want justice. I was drawn away and enticed. All it takes is the planting of a seed, usually a thought that manifests to a deed. I was second guessing and stressing and not counting my blessings. I seemed to be missing all the lessons. One thing for certain, two things for sure, I got it now and that means war.

REFLECTION

The tears I cry

Everyday

For them

The pain I feel I would wish on no one

The sacrifices I made

The things I had to let go

For them

I would do anything

I wonder if they will ever know

Of my strength

Or

Will they view me as weak

Am I their brave hero

Taking on any and every thing

That tries to get in the way

Or take their place

They have a place

It is theirs

And theirs alone

No one else is welcome there

No one else can dwell there

The sacred place

Created for them

Am I just a summer vacation

A trip to the beach

A spring break get away

A Christmas break

Will they ever really know who I am

Will they ever really know how much I love them

Will they ever really know

My pain

My tears

My frustration

My failures

My victories

My efforts

My blood

My sweat

My love

Will they

I pray one day

They will know my side

They will know my truth

They will know my heart

For now

The struggle continues

The fight forges on

Will they ever really know

LIES

Suppose words were sufficient

Red carpeted escort to plateaus

That extend beyond momentary pleasure

Whispers would unfurl mysteries

Of one's most intimate self

Every utterance captivating

Ushering their auditor to a sanctuary

Of security

Where declarations

Deeply rooted and highly esteemed

Transient tongues cast into whirlwinds

With impulsive proclamations

Unredeemed from time and space

Mitigate the sword within the beast

Cause the false dispatching to cease

MISERABLE

Come 'ere man.
Come on over here.
Yeah. You'll get the job done.
Come on now. Fast as you can.

Come lay with me.
I'm feelin' really bad.
Don't wanna be alone just now.
Come play with me.

It's been broken too many times.
Don't want you in my heart.
Crawl right on in my bed.
You bouta make me feel fine.

Put your hands and mouth all over me.
Don't need no music or candles.
Just do what I tell you to do.
My misery needs your company.

HONESTY

See, I can't stand it when people say, "I don't need anybody" Or, "I ain't got nobody 'cause I don't want nobody". Do you honestly think you're fooling ME? You should think again. I had a glimpse of your last journal entry. The one that told God how you hate being alone. You think no one wants you, but you got it all wrong. Problem is, you aren't being true. Forget the story you tell to the world. What are you saying to YOU about you? Until you can be real with yourSELF? Baby you'll have a hard time being real with everyone else.

LETTERS TO LOVE

Dear Love, I hate you. No. That is not even remotely true.

I've only ever wanted, needed and longed for YOU.

To be enveloped and consumed; I thought you wanted me too.

Dear Love, you hurt me but I forgive you. I hurt you, and I forgive me too.

Letting go of you was hard for me to do. I never really wanted that to tell the honest truth.

Your happiness mattered to me. So I only, truly did it for you.

Dear Love, I remember asking you to fight for me and never let me go.

I was in a dark place and pushed you away when I needed you the most.

You always thought I was so strong, but I was fighting demons and was afraid for it to show.

Dear Love, I lost sight of what was important. I was blinded by lust and lies.

I chased after figments of my imagination set up for my ultimate demise.

I couldn't tell you it was happening because I had been beguiled by their disguise.

Dear Love, if only it were in my power, I would turn back the mighty hands of time.

I would go back to the days where I belonged to you and only you were mine.

We used to hold one another and sincerely whisper that we would always be just fine.

Dear Love, long gone are the days trying to prove who was wrong and who was right.

I could see and feel you growing weary but I didn't have it in me to fight.

I was consumed by darkness. You were my only source of hope, my strength and my light.

Dear Love, you weren't supposed to hurt, but rather heal, restore and make whole.

I was angry with you for a long time because you didn't seem to understand the battle for my soul.

You thought I was selfish, inconsiderate and unthoughtful and eventually you waxed cold.

Dear Love, I sincerely desire to erase every unwise, deliberate or unintentional choice we made.

I wish nothing more than to unravel, undo and withdraw every ounce of your pain.

We have parted ways and now I wish only for your financial, mental, emotional and spiritual gain.

Dear Love, these words may never cross your eyes or be heard by your ears.

I'm truly grateful for every experience we've had together and apart through these many years.

All of my prayers for your unending peace and unspeakable joy are cradled in my tears.

MY SECRET

I pay homage to

The light and love you exude

I relish in your ability

To confidently stand in my presence

As the giant

You are

Not that I am so great

Although I am

I know who I am

I am very aware

Of what emanates from my being

I am connected

Only to greatness

You take exceptional care

In your approach

Your words

While they feed my soul

Leave my flesh to burn

With curiosity

A thought

I have pondered

Without conclusion

To pursue satisfaction

Of the passion my body longs to feel

Do I keep you tucked

In the place I deemed

To belong to you

Romantic flights of fancy

Remain my secret Escape

Where we regularly

Rendezvous

Unbeknownst to you

You stir me

THE UGLY DUCKLING

She completely knew what she was
Capable of absolutely anything
And everything
She conjured up in her mind

She made no assumptions
And longed for nothing more
Than all she had
Enough

She entirely loved who she was
Fully available for the taking
There for only one
Worthy

What she was
What she had
Who she was
Apparently more than anyone could properly maintain

CHRIST MUST

So it's Christmas

And it seems everybody wants a gift

The thing willingly given to someone

Without payment

Or we use people

To do things for us

Because of their natural talent

Like baking sweets

Or preparing treats

Perhaps you need help

Hanging that wreath

Tis the season

We are so eager to say

A quick shift to a downtrodden spirit

When things don't go our way

Would it still be Christmas

Without all decorations desserts and toys

Would it still be Christmas

Without seeing the smiles of

Precious little girls and active little boys

Oh the joy

The carols we sing

The presents we bring

The jingle bells ring

And all the lights bling

Are all for naught

If you don't acknowledge the king of kings

'Twas the night before Christmas but there was no tree

No lights or decorations as far as one could see

No beautifully wrapped presents

None for you and none for me

Would your smile then be as bright as can be

See there was a time when I had much

Materials plenty

Cars

A house

Money

Time shares

Clothes And shoes

I had many

So it wasn't a thing to spread my glee

You see

The true test came when all I had was me

No gifts

No money

No tree

Just me

No lights and no cookies

Just his spirit

And the love that filled me

The joy that spilled out of me

That's what Christmas is all about

Now the gift of love

THAT will make you shout

When you're headed down a wrong path

It makes you reroute

That love has a name

It's above every name

He definitely seeks glory

But not fortune or fame

There was only one reason he was born

One reason he came

To be a gift to all who receive

And choose to take his hand

He wants us all

Every boy girl woman and man

All called to serve a king

Who didn't even have a bed

The son of man

With no place to lay his head

Other kings paid homage

They all offered something

They knew who he was and

No one

Could take that from him

So who is this king

The reason of which I speak

He is the reason for the season

Lowly holy mild and meek

The one with our whole hearts

We should earnestly seek

I heard he was the greatest gift

I wanted to open it

I just wanted a peek

What I found was a treat

Since that day I've been on the edge of my seat

No one can predict the way he operates

You can never quite pin his behavior

He does what he wants

How he wants

When he wants

Because he's sovereign

He's our savior

His name is Jesus

He is the Christ

Just take his hand and give him

Your life

Give him an invite

Give him a try

Your life will not ever be the same

All you have to do is call on his name

That's the sole purpose of why he came

Born to die so we could live

While you make sure your meal is prepared just right

And double check that stockings are nice and tight

As you watch Christmas lights

All bright

As they dance into the night

As you sip your egg nog with that first cookie bite

And stare

At the presents all wrapped and stacked with care

Amidst all that

Be sure Jesus is there

Don't fret or be concerned if you have nothing to give

Here's something to give you a lift

You have a heart

And there's no better present

For the greatest gift

"I am full of sense and still senseless.
I am everything and I am nothing."

-Anita Lorraine

HOSPITAL HORROR

Like a bat outta hell he pulled up in front of my best friend's house. Her name was Evelyn. She was neighbor, but more like a sister. I was scared. I thought I was in trouble. I hadn't gone home after school. There was no way I was going back to that house. I couldn't escape her inquires of what was wrong with me. I didn't want to say. I couldn't even fix my mouth to spit out the words. Finally I blurted out, "my dad raped me, Evelyn"! She stood there for a few moments with her mouth wide open. A blind man could obviously see that she didn't know what to say. I didn't really expect her to say anything. Like, what does one say to that sort of thing? She said she was going down the street to tell my mom. I begged her not to. I was terrified and embarrassed. What if she didn't believe me? She pleaded with me to tell someone. "Nita, you have to tell." Looking into her eyes and hearing the desperate plea in her voice, I knew I had to do something.

I called my aunt Diane. She lived a few blocks away. I wanted to walk to her house. I wanted her to wrap her arms around me. I don't know why I didn't go. I trusted my auntie and I figured I would feel better after I told her what happened. "Oh my God! Dink, you have to tell your mother. You HAVE to tell your mother!" the first time she said it was as if she was still processing what I had told her. The second time she said it with conviction and power. I knew she was right, but I didn't want to. I couldn't face my mom after the spectacle I had made of myself in school the day before. I surely couldn't face her after I told her I didn't want to live with her anymore. She would say it was my fault. She would blame me. My auntie was able to convince me to let her tell my mom. I was okay with that.

Seemingly, seconds after I got off the phone with my Auntie, my dad and mom were sitting outside of Evelyn's front door in the blue

Toyota Previa. I heard them pull up. I think my dad drove in reverse down that one way street. I didn't wait for anyone to come get me. I ran outside where my mother was just walking up onto the porch. She didn't say a word. She held me close and walked me to the van. Once we were both inside my dad peeled off as if he were very late to an important meeting. I asked my mom where we were going. Before she could answer, my dad said, "to the hospital". I had heard his voice when he was angry before. I had heard him raise his voice to me and my brothers many times. I had heard his voice when he was tired. I knew when he was frustrated. I could tell when he was happy. This particular sound, I didn't recognize. I was terrified.

  Every light in the room seemed to be on, as bright as it could possibly get. I was asked to take my clothes off - everything. I watched as each article was placed in its own plastic bag with red lettering. I was given a hospital gown and told to lay back on the bed. Everyone spoke so kindly to me, but seemed to be in some sort of rush. I was uncomfortable. I was embarrassed. I was ashamed. I was scared. I listened to the nurse as she explained to my mother what was about to take place. I cringed at the thought. As I lay there on the bed tears began to stream down my face. My mom held my hand. I'm sure she didn't know what to say, but I know she was praying.

  There was a small table set up next to my bed. It was lined with tubes for blood, vials, long sticks with cotton on just one end, tongue depressors, finger nail trimmers and, small baggies with red lettering like the ones I had watched them put my clothes in. There was also a speculum. My heart began racing and the tears continued to stream. I was introduced to a lady from the Crime Victim's Center. Her name was Marleen Miller. My mother was asked to leave. I was left with Marleen and the nurse. "Anita, can you tell me what happened"? I shook my head left to right. She assured me that I didn't have to say, right then, but that eventually I would have to talk about it.

The nurse began explaining what she was about to do. I saw her lips move but I could hear no words. I watched as she pulled out the stirrups and gestured for me to place my feet in them. I cried harder. I wanted my mommy. Seeing my discomfort, Marleen asked if she could hold my hand. She wasn't my mom, but at the moment she was all I had and I squeezed her hand with all my might. I remember the nurse trying to get me to relax and just let my legs fall into a wide open position. I resisted, knowing the doctor was about to stick that thing inside of me. She did her best to make me feel at ease - the nurse. Once the doctor had it secured he took the large q-tip looking stick and swirled it around inside. I didn't feel it, thanks to the discomfort of the speculum. I wondered how they got it to stay in place. I didn't like it all. I wanted it out of me.

I watched as they took the large q-tip and put it in a tube. Then, in went another. It too was placed in a tube and sealed. The doctor stuck his fingers inside of me and pushed my abdomen with his other hand. I didn't like any of it. It didn't feel good. It didn't arouse or stimulate me in any kind of way. I felt terribly invaded. No one asked me if I wanted this. I did not consent to this treatment. I was beginning to feel like someone's science project. I was poked and pricked and pressed for what seemed like an eternity.

From head to toe I was examined and sampled. Once the speculum was removed my pubic hair was combed and several hairs were snatched out at the root with tweezers. The hair on my head was combed over a large zip lock bag with red lettering. Upon completion of that, individual hairs were plucked from my scalp, also with tweezers and placed into a much smaller baggie. All 10 fingers and all 10 toes were scraped underneath the nail. I watched as the scrapings from each nail were wiped into labeled containers. As if being scraped with a metal object weren't enough, they cut all my fingernails and all my toenails. Samples of my skin were scraped off with an abrasive material. Skin from almost every part of my body was taken as a sample. They took my urine. They took my saliva. They even took skin from inside my mouth. My nude body was photographed. No part of me was safe. I had been totally exposed. Inside and out. I was asked questions that I didn't know the answer to in that moment. I felt as if I had done something wrong. I thought they didn't believe me. I just wanted my mom and she was not within my grasp. She couldn't hear me crying? She couldn't feel my heart breaking? She didn't know I didn't want this? She couldn't tell them what they wanted to know? Why didn't she come get me? Why didn't she rescue me from this horror? Did she tell them to do this? All these strangers were in my space and taking things from me that I didn't deem okay. Everything seemed to be happening so fast but at the same time moving in slow motion.

    With the last specimen collected, I was informed that it was okay for me to put my clothes back on. Before I could ask for her, my mom came in and held me. I cried in her shoulder and I didn't want her to let me go. The world that I thought I was prepared for showed me a side of itself that I was not ready for. The world that beckoned to me and told me I could make my own decisions had turned its back on me. The world that told me it had all the answers to my teenage trials was not present to catch my tears or answer my questions of why it had abandoned me. I had only my mother. She was there from day one and in that moment, I knew she'd be there for me til her last breath, even if it were just the two of us.

    Just when I thought it was safe to exhale, a middle aged white man dressed in a police uniform came in and explained something to me. I do not recall a word he said. I can only assume, based on the events that followed, that he was telling me what was about to transpire next. Maybe he wasn't even talking to me. He could have been talking to my mother. "Who called the cops?" I thought. Why did they have to be there? What did I do? Was I in trouble? I couldn't seem to quiet my thoughts and found myself once again, in tears. I was scared. I didn't know what was happening. I couldn't fathom the chain of events I had set into motion earlier that day. Surely, had I known, I probably would not have uttered a word. I would have found a way to cope.

Soon after we left the hospital, I found myself in the back of a police car, sitting across the street from my dad's place. I couldn't imagine why we were there. Perhaps had I focused on the nice officer's words I would know? Alas, I hadn't paid attention, but there I was. The things that happened next can only be described as devastating and confusing. My mother and I were let out of the car and escorted to the sidewalk where my dad, Daryl was waiting with another officer. My father, Carl, was on the porch with several of my other relatives.

I wondered if they knew why we were there. I wondered if it mattered to them that I hadn't come home from school. I wondered why he didn't tell my mom I didn't come home. I wondered if he had told my family what he did. Were they all rallied there for him? So many thoughts flooded my mind and I almost collapsed to the ground trying to figure it all out. I remember hearing my mom and dad arguing with my relatives. I don't recall hearing my father's voice and I was afraid to look at him. I had cousins on the porch who were yelling at me in tones I had only ever heard us take with "outsiders". We didn't talk to each other like that. We only ever fought FOR each other. The tables had somehow turned and now we were at one another's throats, almost literally.

I walked inside the house with two officers, one was ahead of me and the other was behind me. I desperately wanted to leave. Once we were clear of everyone, I walked the officers to the room where I had slept. I pointed out the things that belonged to me and where the "incident" occurred. My life had suddenly turned into something I had only seen on television. There was a photographer and other people with specially marked containers and bags. It was a crime scene and I was the one who died.

Once I was safely back outside with my mom I just wanted to leave. I can't put a definition to what I felt. I only know I wanted go as quickly as possible. Words of anger and accusation continued to be exchanged between my parents and other relatives. Suddenly, all were hushed by the sight of several police officers leaving the house with all of my things, plus the mattress I had slept on the night before. I knew in that moment exactly why we had gone back. Things began to make sense. I was beginning to put the pieces to the puzzle together. As the officers vacated the porch with my belongings it all began again, but at once everything quieted. I only knew my family was still arguing because their mouths were still moving and the expressions on their faces were anything but loving and I was the cause. My dad was escorted back to his vehicle while my mother and I were escorted back to the police car. I never looked back.

Thinking it was finally over, I found myself at place other than home. It was the police station. I don't know how I gathered the strength or courage to proceed, but there I was. I didn't know where to begin. I didn't know how to begin. What was I supposed to say to them - the police? I was instructed to sit down at an officer's desk. His name was Officer Chesco. Seemingly from nowhere, Marleen appeared again. Before coming to join me at his desk, he said a few words to my parents and they walked away. He walked into his office and closed the door behind him. Once again, I just wanted my mom and all I had were these two people I had only known for several hours.

Marleen took my hand and told me that the time had come for me to tell what happened. Her hands were soft and her voice was gentle. She rubbed my back as my eyes swelled with tears. I choked them down as the officer cleared his throat. "Anita, we can go at your pace, but I need for you to tell me everything that happened to you. Don't leave anything out. I know how difficult this must be, but the sooner you get it out, the sooner we can get you home to your mom." I looked into kind eyes of the officer who had been assigned to record my story. I took a deep breath, and I began the detailed account everything that transpired.

Ironically, as I relived that terrible experience, I didn't shed one tear. When Officer Chesco was satisfied, he opened the door and called for my parents. He told them that he had never seen such a display of strength from anyone who had just been through what I had. I didn't feel anything about it at the time, but now, I know it was only prayer that got me through those hard moments and I am eternally grateful to have had people praying my strength.

Although that was just the beginning, I remember every detail of that journey which began over 20 years ago. I remember every hearing and every courtroom. I remember every trip to the District Attorney's office. I can account for every trip I had to make to the Crime Victim's Center for therapy. I remember being haunted by the stories of some of the other girls there. I can call to my mind scanning the courtroom and seeing faces of both sides of my family, but having to look at my dad and point him out in front of a judge as the man who raped me. I remember seeing the case folder with the list of charges. Rape was not among them. I felt cheated. Why had I gone through all that and the charge didn't even stick. I learned that a deal had been made and that particular charge was taken off the table. I remember still wanting my dad in my life. I remember seeing him on the street and running up to hug him. I remember in that moment how I wished I hadn't said anything. I wanted things to be normal. I loved my father. I still do. I remember getting married when I was 19 and visiting him in prison. I remember every letter we exchanged while he was there. I remember the void I felt in my longing to see my siblings and couldn't. I remember some of the most difficult moments in my life were had on that journey and endured without my mom being there in the moment. She wasn't allowed to be. Thank God for my Grandmom. I remember having to take a "morning after pill". I remember my mom explaining it would keep me from getting pregnant. I remember how I got sick to my stomach when she said it. I remember everything. I hate hospitals.

GREATER

Greet each day with thanksgiving and praise

Rise from despair and gather every thought that strays

Empowerment comes from the Word and in prayer

Align every deed with HIS will, surely He is there

Touch and impact lives of many with all you say and do

Every encounter is of utter importance not just a few

Realize GREATER is not coming, but that it lies in YOU

FALLING HIGH

From the moment I was graced with your essence

I've fought to maintain an erect position

Searching for adequate terminology to veil my exposition

Tugging at the curtains to the window of my soul to shield my true disposition

I can be a woman of many words but I always find myself speechless

Grasping at words and moments to thoroughly impeach this

Feeling I can't describe with words though I search because they evade me

Faculties of thinking in disarray I'm caught in a whirlwind that persuades me

Both vulnerable and guarded and it's driving me crazy

Blissfully I dismiss the pull and squeeze in my chest

I'm breathless but ironically not in distress

Upright on my feet feels more like my knees

I'm planted on the ground and walking on trees

Overly intoxicated with no desire to be inoculated

Released of insecurities I anticipate the future and suddenly fears dissipate

No need to exaggerate this is the true state of my heart

Now and forever connected to your most inner part

Intertwined spirits knitted at the soul

Love has a grip and it's a hell of a hold

Too strong to be weak too weak to be strong and I'm all in

Can't stand in your presence 'cause I'm slain by your essence I'm falling

ONCE UPON A TIME

I met you at the station

Our eyes locked

I felt you read my soul

I quickly turned away

I blushed

Embarrassed at what I thought

You saw in my head

A kiss without resistance

A flame ignited

Fiercely burning

Fire coursed through my veins

You eagerly fed it

I know it was aflame in you as well

Your touch

Was like electricity

High voltage

I was left in shock

But I'll never forget your name

LIAR, LIAR

Promises of forever, broken

Vows of commitment, Betrayed

Whispers of eternal passion, Vanished

Cards dealt and hearts played

Windows of the soul, shattered

Foundation, built on sand

Solid home suffered damages

Declarations and decrees didn't stand

PHILLY

I've always been attracted to the city. The lights that brighten the sky on the scrapers at night. The sound of honking horns and trains in transit. The dull roar of the crowd's conversations. The aroma of food drifting from various shops and residences. The kids at play in the middle of the street. Boys playing basketball with a crate fixed to a phone pole. Girls jumping Double Dutch. City noise. Streets lined with stores that have shoes and weave and everything in between. Interesting hair dos and outfits that make me question, "what were YOU thinking when you got dressed today?"

I've been in the city on numerous occasions for a variety of reasons. I never took the time to stop and appreciate all the things that draw me... Until today. I took a train to Center City. I walked only a few blocks from the station on Market to Cherry, then, down 15th. I had no time to stop on my way to my destination. On my way home however, I slowed down my brisk walk to a stroll.

I stopped to watch an elderly man dressed in a navy blue and fire engine, red jogging suit. He was dancing to hip hop music. It was a song I didn't know, but it seemed to be very popular amongst the younger onlookers. He was decked out from head to toe. He wore a blue skully with red trim. He wore red glasses with lightly tinted lenses. His jogging suit was trimmed in red which made his red accessories more noticeable.

I think his red Nikes with the blue swoosh made him feel light on his feet. His body knew the language of the music and spoke it fluently. He looked to be in his early 70s but he moved as if he were just a young lad. I smiled and walked away as he continued to woo the crowd.

There were several street vendors with carts that smelled utterly divine. I inhaled deeply as I passed each one. The first smelled of fresh fruit and other healthy vittles. It made me long for a fresh garden salad with a tall glass of cranberry juice and a side of pineapples. The next few smelled of grease and yummy seasonings. There is nothing like the smell of a Philly Cheesesteak. I could FEEL myself getting fat just taking in the fragrance of all those hot, meat and cheese sandwiches. I wanted one of those too. Delightful was the smell of the fresh, hot, soft pretzels. I could even smell the mustard being squeezed on top of one customer's pretzel. Of course, I wanted one of those as well.

Quite stirring was the sound of the voices of the vendors, beckoning the passersby to stop. Although extremely tempted, I resisted the urge and continued my stroll. By the time I had passed all the carts, my nostrils had been overwhelmed with aroma. I wanted them all, but again, I just smiled and walked away.

It was a beautiful day – stunningly beautiful. The way the light from the sun reflected off the glass of the tall buildings I beheld, made 56 degrees feel more like 68. There was not a cloud in the sky. I found a small, unoccupied bench. I walked over and sat down. I carefully watched the people around me. Some were engaged in cell phone conversations. Some were conversing with one another as they traversed the streets. Others looked dazed and confused like they were trying to figure out how they had gotten to where they were. Some were engrossed in whatever sound emanated from their headphones and ear buds. People everywhere seemed to be glued to their devices. I was curious as to how they got around without having to look up.

As I continued to observe, I noticed that everyone was doing something. So, for just a few moments I did nothing. I clutched my bag tightly, closed my eyes and let the sun's rays wash over my face. Not a thought. Not a care. I just basked in the beauty of the moment God had given me. I opened my eyes, thanked Him for such a beautiful day, pulled out my notebook and began to write.

INTO LIGHT BEFORE DEATH

Water rushes in
I feel your breath on my neck
My heartbeat quickens

A gentle caress
Fingers dance across my skin
I inhale deeply

Breathing your essence
Paralyzed by your presence
Breath escapes my lips

I open my eyes
My soul's secret is unveiled
Resuscitate me

Trapped in a moment
No longing to be set free
Two hearts connected

Sun gives way to moon

We pay homage with our song

Consistent rhythm

Calculated thrusts

Unchoreographed motion

Orchestrated act

La petit mort pleased

You captured my falling corpse

Neglect will to cease

Resuscitate me

The taste of your mouth is life

Breath escapes my lips

Your cry delights me

You're accepted in my walls

With a firm embrace

I feel your end near

Driving yourself deeper in

We whisper last words

Prepared for the crash

Our bodies collide once more

Water rushes in

PHANTOM

I used to hold something special
Now it isn't there.

I let it go like it was nothing
Without a worry or a care.

It haunts me at random moments
Usually when I'm alone.

I'll never know the blessing
You would've been in my home.

THE DEMON THAT STARTED IT

There was a time when it seemed everybody and they mama lived at Grandmom's house. It was a big house. It seemed there were always more people in the house than those who lived there. People were coming to pick up their kids or their pies. In some cases it was both. It always had two distinctive scents. Either is smelled like food, or bleach. Cooking or cleaning was always happening at 842. Each family had their own room. My and mommy's room was directly at the top of the stairs. At the time we only had one bathroom. I loved taking baths. We had a big, white, deep, cast iron bath tub with paws. On occasion, mommy would bathe me and two of my older cousins together. We girls had so much fun in the tub. Well, I did anyway. Sometimes we sang or played hand games. I remember the echo in the bathroom. I liked it.

There is one cousin of whom my memories are not so fond. I used to call him Demon. He wasn't biologically related. He was several years older than me. He was foul, but also very intelligent. When I was about 7 or 8 he would lure me and one of my younger cousins into the bathroom with all sorts of neat toys. Some of which glowed in the dark. He told us that he had to turn the lights off to show us how they worked. He closed both doors to the bathroom and out went the lights. We could see the dimly lit toys in our older cousin's hand. We heard the lid to the seat slam down on the toilet. We followed the tiny lights over to him as he waved them around. He sat us both on each of his legs and gave us a toy.

With our hands full of glow-in-the-dark gadgets, his hands were free to roam our underdeveloped bodies. He started with his hand on my shoulder. I imagine that what he was doing to me with his right hand, he also did to my cousin with his left. He moved his hand from my shoulder to my flat chest. I could feel my heart begin to race as he roughly dragged his hand back and forth, then, down to my waist. He, paused there. I wanted to look at my cousin, but I was too afraid to turn my head. I could feel my eyes widening as they attempted to adjust to the darkness. Feeling his hot, rough hands on my little thighs, I continued to play with the toys in the dark. I could feel my dress being hiked up. I had never been touched like that, but I knew it wasn't right. Still, I played. Pretending that I wasn't feeling what I felt, I turned my head to look at my cousin, but it was too dark for me to see her face clearly. I swallowed hard when I felt his fingers rub my delicate underwear. He kept rubbing and occasionally he would squeeze. My body was too small for him to get a handful, so it felt more like a pinch.

    I had watched Grandmom make bread lots of times and I knew what kneading looked like. At that moment, I understood what it felt like. Dissatisfied with feeling just the ruffles on my panties, he pulled them to the side. I tried to close my legs but his leg was between mine. When he felt that, he started talking to us. He asked if we were having fun with the toys. Neither of us spoke. He began going on about where he got them from. All the while his fingers walked all over my fragile privates. He managed to get his fingers in there. I did not like what he was doing. His fingers felt rough against me. As his fingers wiggled back and forth, the delicate folds of my tiny labia were pinched. He continued to rub for what seemed like forever.

    Finally, we were rescued. I heard my mom's voice from down stairs. My cousin and I jumped up quickly. Damon turned the light on. He spoke quietly – so as not to let anyone hear him but us. He told us that we better not tell anyone. He said that no one would believe us and that we would get a beating for lying. He opened the door, took the toys from us and walked out. I took my little cousin by the hand and we left the bathroom and ran downstairs to my mom. I never told her until I was grown.

When I was 10, I was allowed to go to Ash Park by myself. I went there for one thing, that was to swim. I have always loved the water. I stayed at the pool all day. Some days I was there from open to close. My mom would make surprise visits to make sure I was where I said I would be. Thank God I was always there. I shudder to think of what would happen had I not been. I would only get out to use the bathroom. It seemed like everyone in the city knew my mom. So I'm sure she had eyes on me though she was not physically present. I was a well behaved and honest child and my mother trusted me. I've lied on her and about her, but never TO her.

One day in the summer of '91 I was at Ash Park. It was so hot. It felt like an oven baking a sweet potato pie. There wasn't a cloud in sight. The ice cream truck circled the block several times with its siren blaring. The sound of children and youth laughing and screaming of fun fill the air. People had super soakers and water guns. We had come from all over; Coates St, Oak St, Regency, West End and East End.

There were a few older gentlemen there picking them up and tossing them around in the water. I knew one of them. My grandmom used to babysit him. So I asked if he would throw me too. He signaled for me to jump in the water. Off I went into the cold water. I was having a great time. Laughing and playing with the other kids. One of the guys that I didn't know picked me up to throw me into the deeper waters. The first few times I didn't take notice to what he was doing. I was enjoying the game. I was skinny as a rail in my youth. It was nothing for me to be picked up by these muscle bound men, overhead. I can remember him picking me up and pretending that he suddenly couldn't get me up. He would pick me up with one hand on my thigh and the other on my back. Each time he would go to lift me out of the water, his fingers slipped into the crevice of the bottom piece to my bathing suit. When I caught on to this, I quit the game. I tried to stay away from him in the pool. Unlike a lot of the other kids, I was a great swimmer. I tried to stay in the deeper part of the pool, but all my friends were at the other end. He followed me around and made subtle comments about how nice my swimsuit was. He kept gesturing for me to come to him, wanting to throw me into the deep. I told him I didn't want to play anymore.

Each time I experienced something negative, I internalized it. I blamed myself for wearing a two piece bathing suit. I was mad at myself for being so easy to be picked up. How is it when we encounter things of an unfavorable nature, we figure there has to be something "wrong" with us? Why is it never the other parties involved who has the defect? I was ELEVEN! There was nothing "wrong" with me, or the fact that I wore a two piece bathing suit.

I had memorized his face and his trunks. I left the pool. I didn't head straight home. I went to the police station. I remembered the talks I had with my mom about not allowing anyone to touch my body. My mom said, "If it FEELS wrong, then it IS wrong". I don't know why I went to the police station. I didn't know what they would do about me saying someone touched me. I mean, after all, it was just a touch. I remember having the same ill feeling when my previously mentioned cousin touched me. I intended to go home and not breathe a word of it to my mother or anyone else. I believe that day my footsteps were guided by the Lord. It was a setup for what He knew would happen later in my life. As I walked to the police station, I felt like my feet had 20 pound weights on them. The sky that was so clear and blue had turned cloudy. The sun that was so warm and strong, gave way to a cool breeze. Before I knew it I found myself in the back of a police car on my way to 842 Coates St. with an officer to pick up my mother. We went back to Ash Park, but he was not there. We drove around for a while looking for the bald man with the beard who wore grey swim trunks with an orange stripe down each side. We didn't find him that day. We headed back to the station where I gave a full account of the events of my day. I learned that day that after 5 years, if he wasn't found, nothing could be done. It's called a Statute of Limitation.

I saw that same man several months later in church. He was an usher at a church we were visiting. He couldn't have recognized me. Or, perhaps he didn't think he did anything inappropriate. I said nothing.

Everyone has a story. Mine is one of continuous sexual abuse. I suffered at the hands of boys and men who said they loved me; said they would look out for me; were supposed to protect me; males who were supposed to defend me and come to my aid when I was in trouble. Fortunately for me, I had a mother who was very interested in everything that happened to me. She educated me on hard and uncomfortable subjects like the "good touch, bad touch" and what to do if ever someone took advantage of me sexually. Unfortunately, that day came several times. I did what I knew to do in most cases, but had I known the complete ramifications of my choices, I'm not 100% certain I would make the same decisions.

When I told my mother of the things that happened to me -good or bad- it was no problem for her to believe me. I am blessed to have the mother I have. I can't imagine what going through such ugly things would have been like without her support. She never blamed me or made me feel like I did something wrong. I spoke and she executed. Everyone should have a mom like mine. One who believes them, believes IN them and fights for the best for them. That is not everyone's story and only in a perfect world would it ever be. I have the best mom ever. My prayer is that one day, my children will be able to speak the same of me without ever having to endure the things I have.

A PACKAGED DEAL

Face. Masked

Make up. Flawless

Heart. Broken

Smile. Dazzling

Spirit. Wounded

Stride. Perfect

Walk. Falling

Wardrobe. Top-of-the-line

Armor. Bottom shelf

Shoe game. On Point

Footing. Unsure

That is me.

Perfectly imperfect and perfectly tip toeing around the unperfected edges of my voids.

Careful not to disturb all the empty contents.

Filling them insatiably and growing ever weary

Feeling it all. Smelling it all. Tasting it all. Seeing it all. Hearing it all.

Everything that is and everything that is not.

I am full of sense and still senseless. I am everything and I am nothing.

SELF DESTRUCTION

Fear of rejection paralyzed
Thoughts of failure sterilized

Deprived of success
By feelings of inadequacy

In pursuit of happiness
Never bothering to ask for help

Battling lusts of eyes
And lusts of flesh
That thing called pride had me killing
Myself

Always taught to be strong
Can't appear weak

STILETTOES

Like a Phenomenal Woman, still I rise. I hold my head high knowing where my secret lies. No longer bound by guilt, hurt, shame or pride I hold my head to the sky. I look to the hills. From there comes my help. It was nobody else, but God. I couldn't have done it myself. He made me a warrior, a fighter and queen. He's kept me through dangers seen and unseen. I'm a special being.

There's no denying, I'm definitely blessed. My hands have been caressed and finessed by the Master. I can whip you up a delicious pie, make you a fitted dress, give your hair a press and curl or write eloquent words that will leave you impressed. I don't stress. I just rest in knowing that when God made me, he created the absolute best. No, that doesn't mean I'm better than you. It simply means, what I've been assigned, only I can do. It's the truth and the same goes for you.

I used to have to wear jean skirts and T-shirts because I wasn't allowed to wear pants in church. I remember those long walks up the street in my skirt that passed my knees in my white sneaks. Mommy was one of the youth leaders and I didn't have a choice. When it came to church I didn't have a voice in the matter. It seemed we were always there. Monday thru Saturday, all day Sunday and all I wanted was one free day.

Walking up "the ave" to the place where my mom taught me how to play the tambourine. I learned the bible and how to dance and sing. I sat on the back row just waiting for a chance to get in that side aisle and give a little footwork before the word. In that church on the hill I witnessed people roll under the pews and lose shoes and speak in tongues as the spirit moved. I looked forward to Sunday School. I remember youth meetings and retreats and trips to the beach and watching the saints wash each other's feet. I liked church. It wasn't a bad place to be. There was never a dull moment and always something interesting to see.

So now I wear what I want and do what I like. My style is unique and I think I'm kinda fly. The garments I put on my body are to please my own eyes. So when you see me I'm well put together. I'm a treasure and you really don't know of the storms I've weathered. I've laughed and smiled when I wanted to scream and cry but it all made me better. I'm bigger, not bitter because I learned to rise above it all. I've journeyed to hell and back and I learned to love it all.

To know where my secret lies you need only look into my eyes. You can't tell by my smile. It's deceptive 'cause some things I'm hiding. There were times when inside I was crying and some days I was dying. I want people to look past what they find on the outside. Look into the place where I cannot hide. The windows to my soul will let you know when you're hot or cold.

I have stories never told and lessons learned that never get old. One consistent strand in the fabric of my life is that I never fold. I've been bent and bruised but I never broke. I'm still here. I'm still standing. I tried to quit many times but only proved I don't know how to do that. Something you're facing, I've probably been through that. I was built for this - thought you knew that.

I'm the queen of new beginnings. Starting over is the story of my life but I'm rewriting it now because I didn't like the other endings. I was always picking up broken pieces trying to make myself whole. I needed healing for my soul. I was on a roll, spiraling downward. I was out of control. I attempted to fill all my voids and only made a bigger mess, I tried everything from weed and alcohol to cigarettes and sex. I wanted to be more but I felt like less and people only seemed to be impressed with the way I dressed.

There was a serious spiritual disconnect. Nobody could tell I was depressed. I was internally bleeding with shallow breathing and my heart barely beating. Nobody noticed that but often asked what I used on my skin or admired whatever my feet were in. I've always had a thing for a bad shoe with a steep heel. I wasn't trying to hide behind my looks or mask what I feel. What I needed was a moment to be real in the place designed for me to heal.

I kept having to pour when I needed to be filled. So I became a master of disguise contributing daily to my own demise. I like my heels high because I feel closer to the sky and when I don them I'm reminded to rise. Out of dirt and dust and mud and muck I'm reminded to keep stepping so I don't get stuck. No matter where I go there's someone who adores them. They never know how many times I've scraped, scuffed or tore them. I nod with a polite "thank you" but think to myself, "You only like my stilettoes because you haven't worn them".

PASSION AND PAIN

  I honestly thought I truly loved myself. I used to think I wasn't enough of anything. So, in hindsight, thinking I loved myself enough is laughable. I couldn't possibly have loved myself. I never spent enough time with myself to truly know myself. I knew what made me tick, but I didn't know the whys. I knew the whens, but I didn't know the hows. I never invested the time in myself to answer those questions. I didn't know myself because I didn't like myself and I didn't like myself because I didn't know myself. I didn't know how to embrace what I perceived as substandard regarding me. I was too tall to be short but not tall enough to be considered that. I was too light to be dark but not enough to be light skinned. I didn't have a learning disability but I wasn't smart enough to be gifted. I seemed to never be enough of anything to be considered something. I was always in the middle and thought of myself as average. Internally I felt I never measured up, emotionally, spiritually and mentally. I didn't have the proper units of measurement and I refused to think I could be more even though I wanted it. I didn't love myself enough to pursue it. I settled for mediocrity and failed to embrace and appreciate every quality that made me, me.

  I have always poured into others. I did so willingly but with an expectation of validation. I was always waiting for someone else to tell me who I was. Affection was always at their discretion and time at their allotment. Yet, I was always there, eagerly waiting to consume words with which I could build my own esteem. Often I was left wanting. I was so busy being with the ones I loved, I forgot to love the one I was with – ME. So readily I pushed others ahead of myself. I found delight in fully investing myself in the advancement of everyone but me. I looked on with a smile that patched a broken heart as their visions were fulfilled. Mine had become mere shadows in my dreams. My tears were a mixture of joy and sorrow. I did it for everyone else, but never gave myself permission to be great.

I had to learn that other people's inability to handle the weight of my identity doesn't diminish my value. Their failure to recognize the beauty of my free spirit in no way depreciates the worth of my personality. I am powerful beyond measure. I am an unlimited force. In me lies the ability to heal creation, birth a nation, bring revelation and inspire reconciliation. My words are gifts to the universe. They are creative and powerful. I have not always appreciated or honored their place in my life. I have at times abused their purpose.

It was unfair to place the burden of all that is me on the shoulders of others. I couldn't allow them to completely love me because I didn't completely love myself. I couldn't receive because I didn't know how.

Somewhere in my mind I wasn't supposed to be great. It was selfish for me to push myself to achieve better. It was greedy of me to want more for myself. I wasn't supposed to shine. That's what I thought. Little did I know, not living up to my greatest potential is a slap in God's face. He is the Creator and he created me. Deliberately choosing not to be what he predestined me to be caused me to live a life that was void of purpose. I was just a shell of what was intended by my maker. Isaiah 45:9 (KJV) speaks of "him that striveth with his maker". The clay doesn't question the potter. Its entire purpose is to be whatever the framer fashions it to be, in whatever way it is fashioned. I used to question God all the time as to why he "made me this way". Through his silence I have learned the answer to that question. It wasn't apparent to me in the lesson. I didn't feel it in the tender words he spoke to me. I didn't hear it in what I read in his word. I didn't find it in the words of encouragement offered to me by others. I found the answer in the most unlikely place. It was revealed during the most unlikely time. It was in the test. I found the answers I needed when he wasn't speaking. They had been inside of me all along. I needed only to look inside myself.

This journey hasn't been about finishing a project. It wasn't about disclosing my heartbreaks or sharing my intimate encounters. It wasn't about exposing my abuse. It wasn't the pouring out of my heart's secrets. This journey hasn't been about my failed relationships or attempts to soothe gaping voids. This voyage into me wasn't about telling of my failures, struggles and insecurities. It's not even about my victories and triumphs over the things that once held me captive. That was the purpose of sharing the process. So what was it? What was the purpose of the journey?

This entire trip has been about love. It was both the source of my passion and my pain. It is the one thing I have always longed for. It is the thing that drives me. It is what guides me and inspires me. It is what sustains me. It's so powerful, the pursuit of it almost literally killed me. I was chasing something and waiting for something I wasn't prepared for. I needed to learn to love myself. Before I could fully receive everything I thought I wanted, I had to completely accept everything that is me.

I used to stare at myself in the mirror for hours with tears in my eyes. I would wonder why the coils of my not quite black hair were so tight. I couldn't understand why my eyes were the color of dark chocolate. Why did God give me skin the color of honey roasted peanuts? I thought I was the only girl in the world who snores. Pretty girls don't snore. Pretty girls don't have nappy hair. Pretty girls have fair skin. Everything I had ever been teased about became a target of my own disdain. I hated all the things about myself that I couldn't change. Self-hatred was destroying me.

Until this journey, I had never been in a position to fully receive or reciprocate love in a manner that was healthy and satisfying to mind, body and soul in myself or others. My perception and interpretation of love was jaded. Life had taught me that it was conditional and circumstantial. There was something I had to do or be in order to receive in a manner I thought was appropriate. When it was freely offered void of ill motive and intention, I rejected it. I had grown accustomed to and accepted the way others demonstrated love. However they defined it or deemed me worthy to receive, I took it. At whatever capacity they shared, when I wanted or needed more, I never challenged for fear they would leave. Guess what? They left anyway.

Several times over I had to teach my heart not to want what it can't have. It is a lesson yet to be learned. My heart refused to believe it couldn't have the one thing it was created for. So I was inspired to hope against hope that one day I would receive the love I desperately longed for. I would not have to chase it. I would not have to change anything about myself to gain its approval. It would not look beyond my faults, but rather challenge me to be better. Love would not fail me and it would not allow me to fail.

I was looking for perfection. I was expecting it. I have been looking for love and that is exactly who I found - God. My heart longed for its creator. It ached to be massaged by his omnipotent hands with a tender touch only he could yield. The love I sought could not be found in flawed creatures. It could only come from a place that is divine. I was never truly satisfied because I placed a burden on imperfect beings to fill a space that was designed for God to dwell. No man or woman or deed would ever have been enough.

I had to be taught how to receive love. It was a lesson only God could teach, and only when I was ready. Now that I love myself, it is so much easier to receive from everyone else. I am no longer afraid of losing anyone or anything. I am able to appreciate love in every form it is offered to me. I am thankful for those who love me, and for those who don't. I have gleaned from both sides of that fence. It doesn't change who I am. I no longer feel the need to force my square in anyone's circle.

I am completely accepted and loved by Elohim. He is the Creator. He made me the way I am, yet daily I strive to be better. I long to walk closer. I desire to go deeper. His love is amazing. His grace is truly sufficient. It enables me to supernaturally do all the things I can't do of my own accord. I can't get enough of him. Each time I think of straying, he gently, but powerfully reminds me of what I have in him. He is my passion and he has taken away my pain.

THE END

AFTERWORD

Every now and then a literary work comes along that has the ability to transport you from your present reality directly into its pages. In Anita Lorraine's 52 Weeks of Passion and Pain, she takes readers on an emotional roller coaster, from beginning to end. The destination of endless possibilities serves as the vehicle of this creatively crafted story, as it unveils one's own undeniably hidden combination of the two. From faith, family and fear to sin, sorrow and seed, she comes face to face with the realities of life – and the mountains that formed as a result. In addition to encouragement and inspiration, readers will be confronted head on with issues one generally chooses to "sweep under the rug". Her 52 week journey will assist you as you go through your own ups and downs of life.

Pastor Dana Berry

CEO/Founder

Dana Berry Ministries

Executive Pastor

Celebration Church of Detroit

www.ingramcontent.com/pod-product-compliance
Lightning Source LLC
Chambersburg PA
CBHW032047090426
42744CB00004B/118